"AND I WILL ESTABLISH MY COVENANT BETWEEN ME AND YOU AND
YOUR DESCENDANTS AFTER YOU IN THEIR GENERATIONS. . . ."
GENESIS 17:7

THE

MISSION-MINDED

FAMILY

D0109516

Ann Dunagan is the most effective and gifted children's teacher and motivator that I have come across in my lifetime. . . . Let her teach you—listen to her—she knows how and is now sharing it with others.

—Doris Gene Stewart, forty years of experience as a missionary to Brazil and founder of an orphanage

I have known Jon and Ann Dunagan since 1987, and have had the privilege of being their friend, pastor, and fellow worker in the kingdom. . . . Jon and Ann are people of integrity, and I have confidence that God will continue to use them greatly in this generation.

—Pastor Nels Church, director of REAP International and missionary to the Philippines

We sincerely appreciate Ann's willingness to help raise the voice of the persecuted church.

—Myrtle Dodd, The Voice of the Martyrs

Ann Dunagan's writing is for those who want a heavy emphasis on world missions. . . . This book was not whipped up by a novice. The author is an evangelist's wife and homeschooling mother of seven who has ministered in more than twenty countries. She knows her stuff!

—Virginia Knowles, Hope Chest Newsletter

Ann, may the Lord bless you in your publishing of this needed book. . . . We are truly hoping that the Lord will open our children's eyes and hearts to the tremendous harvest field that they may be called to work in someday. I know that living in a Third-World country broadens our perspectives and helps us to see the bigger picture of God's redemptive plan, so that's what we're praying for our children.

—Valerie Shepard, pastor's wife and homeschooling mother, and daughter of Jim and Elisabeth Elliot

THE

MISSION-MINDED

FAMILY

Releasing Your Family to
God's Destiny

ANN DUNAGAN

IVP Books

An imprint of InterVarsity Press
Downers Grove, Illinois

InterVarsity Press
P.O. Box 1400, Downers Grove, IL 60515-1426
World Wide Web: www.ivpress.com
Email: email@ivpress.com

©2007 by Ann Dunagan

All rights reserved. No part of this book may be reproduced in any form without written permission from InterVarsity Press.

InterVarsity Press® is the book-publishing division of InterVarsity Christian Fellowship/ USA®, a movement of students and faculty active on campus at hundreds of universities, colleges and schools of nursing in the United States of America, and a member movement of the International Fellowship of Evangelical Students. For information about local and regional activities, visit intervarsity.org.

All Scripture quotations, unless otherwise indicated, are taken from the New King James Version. *Copyright ©1982 by Thomas Nelson, Inc. Used by permission. All rights reserved.*

Scripture quotations marked NLT *are taken from the* Holy Bible, New Living Translation, *copyright ©1966. Used by permission of Tyndale House Publishers, Inc., Wheaton, Illinois 60189. All rights reserved.*

Scripture quotations marked NIV *are taken from the* Holy Bible, New International Version®. *NIV®. Copyright © 1973, 1978, 1984 by Biblica, Inc.™. Used by permission of Zondervan. All rights reserved worldwide.*

Scripture quotations marked AMP *are taken from the* Amplified Bible, *Copyright ©1954, 1958, 1962, 1964, 1965, 1987 by The Lockman Foundation. Used by permission.*

Scripture quotations marked KJV *are taken from* The King James Version. *Public domain.*

Originally published by Biblica.

ISBN 978-0-8308-5705-0

Printed in the United States of America ∞

 As a member of the Green Press Initiative, InterVarsity Press is committed to protecting the environment and to the responsible use of natural resources. To learn more, visit greenpressinitiative.org.

Cataloging-in-Publication Data is available through the Library of Congress.

P	15	14	13	12	11	10	9	8	7	6	5	4	3
Y	24	23	22	21	20	19	18	17	16	15			

To my wonderful husband:

Jon, it's so awesome going through life with you.
Thanks for marrying me and for being such a great dad
(and now grandpa) to our continually growing family.
Thanks for all the adventures and for living
out your mission-minded motto:

"You can only export what you grow at home."

Look beyond your children's faces
and see the potential of a new generation—
the *families* they will guide,
the *friends* they will lead to Jesus,
and yes, even the *nations* they will impact.

ANN DUNAGAN

Contents

Foreword

Contrary to what some in missions have mistakenly thought, we do not have to neglect our family responsibilities in order to accomplish God's will in our ministry to others. Sacrificing our children on the altar of missions is very close to a modern form of Molech worship, which God continues to abhor. The family is not an obstacle to ministry; it is a vehicle for ministry. But like all road-worthy vehicles, the family must be maintained in order to go the distance and finish its course over a lifetime. And it has been made for the road, not for the garage. It actually becomes stronger and more effective as all of its members devote themselves together as a team for service to others outside the family.

One way of harmonizing the obligations of the family with those of mission is to think of each Christian as an ambassador for Christ and his or her home as an embassy of the kingdom of God. An embassy has gates and schedules. It serves its host nation from a position of strength. It has God-given authority over all of its own interests. But it is intended to be open and accessible by means of routine hospitality. It exists to serve as a display of the goodness and wisdom of God's ways. It is a place where others can literally taste and see that the Lord is good and where the Gospel of the Kingdom is readily proclaimed and explained to all who will listen.

The Mission-Minded Family is an excellent thought-provoking resource to assist Christian families in moving in this more sane and biblical direction. By establishing this balance between our personal lives and our outreach to others we can enjoy a productive mission while launching a new generation into the same missionary lifestyle. By honoring God's wisdom, our families can effectively raise our own children for the Lord, and simultaneously, reach our world with the good news of Jesus Christ.

God is too good and too wise to give us conflicting obligations. Every obligation from God is perfectly compatible with every other obligation that comes from God. Not only are our obligations to family and missions compatible, they are mutually supportive in His purposes. Households united in ministry together provide the best launching pad for a new generation of ministry, because "Whoever walks with the wise becomes wise . . ." (Proverbs 13:20).

As you read *The Mission-Minded Family*, you will be "walking with the wise." Ann Dunagan will walk with you through a very important topic, one that could spare you and your children the heartache that many well-meaning missionary families have had to endure because of shortsighted missionary traditions. With all due respect to their sacrifices, in the end I am confident that you will discover with a growing wave of missionary families that God is indeed good, and that the sacrifices He demands of us as missionaries are compatible with the responsibilities He has entrusted to us as a family. May your own adventure in missions raise up the foundation for many generations of effective service in the Gospel.

—Gregg and Sono Harris

Gregg Harris is a Christian husband (widowed since 2010) and father of seven children. He and his late wife, Sono, were pioneer leaders in the family-restoration and Christian homeschooling movements since 1980. Their children include Joshua Harris (influential author and leader) and Alex and Brett Harris (authors of *Do Hard Things* and founders of www.therebelution.com a "teenage rebellion against low expectations" where young adults are challenged to "do hard things for the glory of God and the good of others").

The Mission-Minded
Family Features

Hymns and Poems

From My Children's Perspective

Mini Missionary Biographies

(those marked with an asterisk include a "Mission-Minded Monologue Skit")

Mission Stories

Teaching Opportunities

How to Use This Book

This book is a tool to encourage your family to become more mission-minded. Every Christian family can participate in helping to expand the kingdom of God, and this book can give you some information—and inspiration—to help!

- **Get inspired!** Browse through the pages for motivating missions stories, hymns, poems, and testimonies. Renew your passion and commitment to reaching the lost. Christ's Great Commission should be our family's mission.

- **Look things up!** This book is a quick resource tool, with examples of missionary family heroes, great mission quotes, and exciting prayer projects.

- **Find practical ideas!** Are you looking for easy-to-use missions ideas? Included are creative prayer projects, mission-minded ministry ideas, and practical tips for international travel—together with one of your children or with your whole family!

- **Impart to your family a passion for missions!** This book is filled with inspiration to help you incorporate a heart for the Great Commission into nearly every aspect of your family life. At the core level, *The Mission-Minded Family* is about establishing a brand-new mindset. As you focus on God and His Great Commission, everything will be radically altered—including your thoughts about the world and those in need, your prayer life, your eating habits (and what you're willing to "try"), your disciplines in health and fitness, your family's stewardship of faith and finances, and your decisions regarding your children's education. A missions mindset will impact—for eternity—your focus on the future.

What Is a
Mission-Minded Family?

Your family may never be called to become missionaries in a foreign country; yet as followers of Jesus Christ, you are still called to be mission-minded. When Christ gave His Great Commission—"Go into all the world and preach the gospel" (Mark 16:15; see also Matthew 28:18–19)—He wasn't just speaking to special apostles, future missionaries, or a few chosen preachers. Jesus was unveiling His purpose for *all* of us. And His words were not just a "Great Suggestion." As Hudson Taylor once said, "The Great Commission is not an option to consider; it's a command to obey."

Jesus fulfilled God's mission for His life. Yet His ministry continues today—through us. In Acts 1:1, Luke described his "former account" (the Gospel he had previously written) as the testimony "of all that Jesus *began* both to do and teach" (emphasis added). Throughout the world today, the Lord Jesus is *still* saving people and changing their lives; and your family can participate in what He's doing.

Instead of merely asking God to bless *your* kids, meet *your* needs, and fulfill *your* personal goals, seek God for how your family can bless *others*, meet *others'* needs, and help fulfill *God's* goals. Rather than praying, "Lord, please bless *our* plans," find and follow *God's* plans—because God's plans are already blessed!

There are no cookie-cutter shapes or standards for mission-minded families. Such families come in all sizes, nationalities, and social groups, simply sharing a common love for the Lord and the lost.

Our mission is the Great Commission, and this focus affects each family member (as an individual) *and* the entire family (as a unit). Mission-minded families love God, they are focused on expanding God's kingdom, and they are some of the happiest people on earth! Here are ten examples of various kinds of mission-minded families:

- **John and Angelique** sit with their children on the front row of our church every Sunday, intensely focused on worship and always eager to learn from God's Word. John is a professional fishing guide, and Angelique is a homeschooling mom and a preschool teacher. John and Angelique minister to the youth in our church, helping with whatever needs done, and they are passionate about missions. For years their family has sponsored children from several missionary organizations, and they recently adopted a little boy they had taken into their home as a foster child. They give generously to international evangelism, and they earnestly pray for the lost, both overseas and within their own family. A few days ago I heard that Angelique was learning "with" her kids about Gladys Aylward (a missionary to China); and John recently traveled on a short-term mission trip to Africa, an effort that focused on preaching, planting a church, baptizing new believers . . . and teaching people to fish!

- **Delbert and Manja** don't fit the typical missionary mold, but they are two of the most intensely mission-minded people I know. They have a blended family, with "his" and "her" kids from previous marriages; and their eating preference is vegan. Delbert works for Google, and Manja grows organic plants and has a face-painting business (painting children's faces for parties and community events). As God has given them a passion for His mission, it has totally changed how their family thinks, speaks, reads, gives, and obeys. God challenged Delbert's attitude in the area of finances, primarily through Randy Alcorn's book *Money, Possessions, and Eternity*. The couple's focus changed from investing and preparing for retirement to making an eternal difference for

Christ. They dedicated an entire year's profits from their face-painting business to sponsor an overseas orphanage, and Manja and her daughter are currently sewing dresses (each one uniquely designed) for one hundred orphan girls. Their hearts are especially burdened by the needs of the Invisible Children ministry in Africa; and to deepen their compassion for displaced people, their family participated in a gathering of five thousand people who slept overnight in self-made cardboard shelters.

- **Bob and Carol** are godly grandparents. Bob was a contractor and pastor of a small country church, and Carol was a home economics teacher. As they approached their golden years, they decided to surrender their retirement dreams to God and obey whatever He asked them to do. The first direction outside of their comfort zone they received was to visit a local bar several times a week. Although they didn't drink alcohol, they started to establish relationships with non-Christians there and began to share the gospel. A few years later they traveled on a short-term mission trip. And today they are full-time overseas missionaries, training thousands of village pastors, operating a large orphanage they founded, training nationals in construction projects and home economics skills . . . and having the time of their lives! Bob and Carol aren't able to see their grown children and their grandchildren as often as they would like; but when they do, they instill a powerful mission-minded heritage!

- **Brent and Virginia** are newlyweds with a passion for God. Growing up, each felt God's call to missions. Brent led a lunchtime Bible club at his public high school, which grew to reach hundreds of students; he wrote English papers about Christian missionary work; and he participated in many short-term mission trips. Virginia felt led to work with a mission organization and ministered for a while in Asia. After getting married, they were hired by a large church to lead a Master's Commission program. Later they felt called to leave this secure position to become full-time missionaries in Africa. Brent and Virginia are enjoying their early years of marriage in Uganda, where they are helping people come to Christ, caring for orphans and the poor, and building churches.

- **Sonja** is a single mom with a ten-year-old son. Five years ago she was unsaved, addicted to drugs, trapped in an immoral lifestyle, and living on the streets of a large city. A friend prayed for her and invited her to church, and God has totally transformed her life. Today Sonja manages a successful daycare business, and she and her son Austin are part of my family's church and home group. Over the past two years Sonja has organized monthly parents' night out parties, with all proceeds (on a donation basis) going to missions. She has purchased uniforms and educational supplies, along with providing financial support, for several missionaries and national ministers. Sonja has also traveled on several mission trips of her own: to Africa, Europe, and Asia. She led craft projects at an overseas orphanage, she shared about God's grace at a church in Japan, and she helped to distribute thousands of Operation Christmas Child boxes in the Philippines through Samaritan's Purse. Sonja has become a happy person and a good mother. She and Austin are preparing to take a mission trip together. With God, nothing is impossible!

- **Aaron and Carol** are just starting their own business. Carol is a former YWAM (Youth With A Mission) missionary, having ministered for six years in Belize, South America, with a special calling for intercession. As a family with five school-age children, Aaron and Carol teach children about the Lord and encourage others (especially young people and women) to have a greater heart for missions. Their oldest daughter, a young teenager, feels a special drawing to international missionary work. Aaron and Carol are nurturing this calling by taking her to a missions "Perspectives" class and training her to pray for the world.

- **Cassie** is twenty-one years old. Though not yet married, Cassie believes that God has called her to be a mother who has a mission-minded family. She has ministered on mission trips to Haiti, Africa, and India, including a YWAM Discipleship Training School where she trained missionary children from throughout Southeast Asia in intercessory prayer. Cassie has ministered to youth and children for years, and she has been a women's retreat speaker alongside her mother. Cassie envisions herself, in the future, leading short-term family mission trips and encouraging others in missions. In the meantime, she is keeping her heart pure, growing closer to the Lord through worship and studying God's Word, and fervently praying for her future husband.

- **Paul and Eleanor** have been in full-time missionary service for over fifty years. They have lived in many countries and have experienced radical testimonies of God's deliverance and provision (especially during wartime). Even in their eighties their hearts overflow with a passionate zeal for God and missions. All five of their grown children are in full-time ministry (as missionaries, pastors, or youth ministers), and their whole family is mission-minded. This past year I attended one of their grandchildren's weddings (the young couple got engaged in Egypt and were already ministering as worship leaders and youth pastors). The anointing and presence of God were so strong as this godly grandfather prayed over the bride and groom. I'm sure everyone in the sanctuary knew this wasn't just about two beautiful young people; this union was focused toward fulfilling God's purpose for the next generation—and there was hardly a dry eye in the audience!

- **Jayson and Julie** have five children, all attending public schools. Jayson is a road excavator and Julie owns a scrapbook store. Over the years, their family has housed foreign exchange students from Hong Kong, Thailand, China, and Italy. One of these students, from China, has gone on to write several influential books in Chinese and was recently accepted into graduate school at Harvard. Because of their family's influence, this young man (who still calls Jayson "Dad" and Julie "Mom") is no longer a Buddhist. He became a believer and now attends a Christian church. Julie recently went to China to meet and share with this young man's family, while Jayson traveled to Africa to share the gospel and use his road-building expertise to build safe pathways on a remote island!

A Mission-Minded Family

A mission-minded family . . . loves to make God smile!

A mission-minded family . . . learns to be diligent, because there's work to be done and many needs in this world.

A mission-minded family . . . brings a stack of well-worn Bibles to church!

A mission-minded family . . . enjoys presents at Christmastime, but never forgets all the poor little children in Cambodia who have nothing.

A mission-minded family . . . is focused on eternity.

A mission-minded family . . . knows how to look up Afghanistan, Bolivia, Singapore, and Tibet, and

imagines more than what they see on a
map.

A mission-minded family . . . eats rice!

A mission-minded family . . . learns how to share the "gospel colors"
and is excited about the miniature
EvangeCube that can hook to a kid's
backpack.

A mission-minded family . . . dreams of traveling around the world and
makes sure each person has an updated
passport—just in case!

A mission-minded family . . . thinks about the Irish on St. Patrick's
Day—and all the people wearing green
who don't have a clue that Patrick was a
missionary.

A mission-minded family . . . lives in SUB-mission!

A mission-minded family . . . shakes missionaries' hands after church
and invites their family over for dinner.

A mission-minded family . . . knows that when the Lord guides, He also
provides.

A mission-minded family . . . keeps the lawn mowed, as a good
Christian witness to the neighbors.

A mission-minded family . . . is strategically aimed for God's purpose.

A mission-minded family . . . anticipates the excitement of the teenage
years and looks forward to youth group
mission trips.

A mission-minded family . . . keeps active and healthy in order to
be physically able to do whatever God
requires.

A mission-minded family . . . gives generously—even when it hurts!

A mission-minded family . . . enjoys carryon luggage with wheels, final boarding calls, and airline peanuts.

A mission-minded family . . . thinks beyond the box of what's merely expected and hopes to do something big (or something little) for God.

A mission-minded family . . . lives for Jesus!

Part I

Our Family and God's Plans

CHAPTER 1

Releasing Your
Family to God's Destiny

God has a destiny for your family. He has an individual plan for each member, as well as a "corporate" purpose for you as a family unit. God will help you, as parents, to train each child toward God's mission for his or her life, and He will help you to focus your family toward making a strong impact for His kingdom—in your community, in your church, in your children's schools, and in the world.

The Bible says in Psalm 127:4, "Like arrows in the hand of a warrior, so are the children of one's youth." This verse recently "hit" me in a new way as I was attending a graduation party. During the evening, a group of church leaders, led by the graduate's father, gathered to pray for this young man. He had been raised to have a fervent heart for God and for world missions, and we prayed for God's purposes to be fulfilled. As I laid my hands on the graduate's mom (my dear friend Karen), I could sympathize with her mixed feelings: happiness and pride combined with a sad realization that this season in their family's life was coming to an end. As we prayed, I "saw" (in my mind's eye) her eighteen-year-old son as a straight arrow in a bow. Afterward, I leaned over and whispered in my friend's ear, "You know, Karen, it's not enough just to aim our arrows; to hit the target we've got to release the string!"

As our children grow, there will be repeated times of releasing each one to God: letting go of a little hand as a baby takes that first wobbly step . . . letting go of total educational control as a child steps onto that school bus or enrolls in that first college course. Or what about that moment when we let go of the car keys and an eager teenager plops into the driver's seat of our car and takes control of the steering wheel?

Sometimes it's very scary.

As I write this chapter, my husband and I have a nearly twenty-year-old son climbing a dangerous mountain and then the following week heading to Oxford, England for a summer-long study-abroad program. Our eighteen-year-old son just graduated from high school and will soon be moving to a university two thousand miles from home. Our nearly sixteen-year-old daughter is just about to get her driver's license.

No matter how many times I have released my children, I continually need to rely on God's fresh grace for today's particular moment. Whether it's dropping off a little one into the arms of a church nursery worker or dropping off a young adult at an international airport, I need to trust God.

Just like Hannah released her little Samuel, I have surrendered each child to the Lord; yet I still have times when God convicts me that I need to rely on Him even more. At a deeper level, I need to *continue* to trust Him. With faith, I need to trust that God will direct each of my kids to fulfill His purposes (without me pushing them to do what I want). I need to trust that God will bring just the right spouse for each of my sons and daughters (without me trying to make something happen). And I need to trust God that He will protect my children as they begin to step out to fulfill His destiny (without me worrying or trying to figure it out).

As I have thought about this need to totally release each of my children to God's purposes, I have tried to imagine—in my own finite way—what our heavenly Father must have experienced when He released *His* Child. God never struggles, but I believe He can relate to my feelings (and yours). He too had to release His Son—His only Son—in order to fulfill His plans for this earth.

Imagine with me:

What if someday God called one of my children . . . let's just say, for an example, to go on a summer mission trip to Calcutta, India?

Would I be able to send him or her with confidence and joy?

If my husband and I prayed about the particular outreach and God gave us His peace about it, I know I would. My husband and I would uphold our child in prayer, and we would trust God's direction. And as a mom, I would rely on Him for grace.

But the sacrifice God made was far greater . . .

What if someday a child of ours decided to *move* to Calcutta, India, for perhaps ten months . . . or ten years . . . or even longer? Could I handle that?

That would be much harder.

Although it would be difficult to live so far apart, I would do my best to support him or her through regular prayer and communication (and I would definitely hope for e-mail access!). If my grown child had a family, I would really miss getting to know my child's spouse and his or her family; and I can hardly imagine how much I would yearn for time with those future grandchildren. Yet, if God was calling my child, I would let my child go . . . and rely on Him for extra grace.

But God's sacrifice was still far greater . . .

So, to take the analogy one step further, what if my husband and I, back in time about twenty years ago, were expecting our first child, and God told us that He wanted us to *surrender* this precious newborn—right from birth? What if God said He had chosen a poor couple in Calcutta, India, to raise *our* baby? What if He said our little one would grow up in some obscure squatter village . . . would live among filth and poverty . . . would spend his life helping people . . . and, in the end, would be rejected, hated, and brutally killed by the very people he was sent to help?

Would I send my son to do that? How could I?

But (perhaps) that is a glimpse of what God did for us.

If we are going to raise a generation of world changers, it is likely that we will need to surrender our children into areas that may make us uncomfortable. He could call our child to pioneer a megachurch in a crowded inner city or to raise a large, God-fearing family in a quiet rural town. He may want our child to impact a corrupt political system or to redirect a greed-motivated business. He could call our precious son to enlist in the military or our pure daughter to have an effect on the media. He could call our child to Cairo, Egypt . . . or to New York City . . . or maybe even to Calcutta, India.

As mission-minded parents, will we "let go" of those arrows and encourage each child to fulfill the Lord's plans? Or will we be God's greatest hindrance?

It's a heart issue, and it's big.

Just as God released His Son for us, we need to totally release each of our children—again and again, every day—for His eternal purposes.

PURSUING GOD'S PURPOSES

An excerpt from *The Missions Addiction*, by David Shibley

We whine, "I just want to know my purpose; I've got to reach my destiny." We race all over the country to attend "destiny conferences," and we devour tapes and books on "reaching your full potential." It would be amusing if it were not so appalling. Even cloaking our self-centeredness in Christian garb and jargon cannot cover the nakedness of this cult of self that has infested much of the church. How can we ever hope to discover our purpose in the earth with little or no interest in His purpose? How will we ever know our destiny when we have so little identification with God's destiny for the nations? It certainly is good to pray, "Lord, what is Your will for my life?" But even this can be a self-absorbed prayer. It is far better to pray, "Lord, what is Your will for my generation? How do You want my life to fit into Your plan for my times?"

Pursuing God's purposes, not our own, is the path to personal fulfillment.

WE'VE A STORY TO TELL TO THE NATIONS

A missions hymn, by H. Ernest Nichol (1862-1928)

We've a story to tell to the nations,
That shall turn their hearts to the right,
A story of truth and mercy,
A story of peace and light,
A story of peace and light.

Chorus:
For the darkness shall turn to dawning,
And the dawning to noonday bright,
And Christ's great kingdom shall come on earth,
The kingdom of love and light.

We've a song to be sung to the nations,
That shall lift their hearts to the Lord,
A song that shall conquer evil,
And shatter the spear and sword,
And shatter the spear and sword.

We've a message to give to the nations,
That the Lord who reigneth above
Hath sent us His Son to save us,
And show us that God is love,
And show us that God is love.

We've a Savior to show to the nations,
Who the path of sorrow hath trod,
That all of the world's great peoples
May come to the truth of God,
May come to the truth of God!

Chorus:
For the darkness shall turn to dawning,
And the dawning to noonday bright,
And Christ's great kingdom shall come on earth,
The kingdom of love and light.

"I have seen the Vision and for self I cannot live;
Life is less than worthless till my all I give."

OSWALD J. SMITH

CHAPTER 2

Three Powerful Dynamics
of a Mission-Minded Family

In a mission-minded family, there's a God-infused energy. There's a focus on God's worldwide purpose. There's a passion for the lost. There's a spiritual depth and hunger that reaches beyond the maintenance mode of cultural Christianity. A mission-minded family emphasizes leadership, calling, and destiny. There's a prevailing attitude of self-sacrifice and an emphasis on total submission to God's will. And there's an unmistakable and contagious joy.

I believe these qualities can be identified and summarized in three powerful dynamics.

Dynamic #1
A Mission-Minded Family Is Focused on Eternity

Mission-minded families have a focused purpose for life. But what is this target? What is our "mission" or our final destination?

In the secular motivational book *The Seven Habits of Highly Effective People*, author Stephen Covey presents a challenge to "begin with the end in mind." He encourages his readers to evaluate their priorities in life by envisioning their own funeral, three years from today:

> As you take a seat and wait for the services to begin, you look at the program in your hand. There are to be four speakers. The first is from your family, immediate and also extended—children, brothers, sisters, nephews, nieces, aunts, uncles, cousins, and grandparents, who have come from all

over the country to attend. The second speaker is one of your friends, someone who can give a sense of what you were as a person. The third speaker is from your work or profession. And the fourth is from your church or some community organization where you've been involved in service.

Now think deeply. What would you like each of these speakers to say about you and your life? What kind of husband, wife, brother, or mother would you like their words to reflect? What kind of son or daughter or cousin? What kind of friend? What kind of working associate?

What character would you like them to have seen in you? What contributions, what achievements would you want them to remember? Look carefully at the people around you. What difference would you like to have made in their lives?

This is an interesting thought. As I've glanced over newspaper obituaries or attended a funeral service, I've often wondered how my life—along with the lives of each member of my family—would someday be summarized. I have heard about a goal-setting project of writing your own obituary, then living your life to fulfill it.

It's good to consider the godly legacy we will leave for the next generation and important to realize that our day-to-day decisions can leave a lasting example, for good or for evil. But as Christians, and as members of mission-minded families, our funeral, or even our godly legacy, is not the end. Our ultimate life evaluation will not be determined by the opinions of those *we leave behind*. Instead, our life will be judged by the One *we go to meet*—our almighty God in heaven.

Because of the death and resurrection of Jesus, and our salvation by grace and through faith in Him, the question of whether our destiny is in heaven or hell is answered. However, the Bible speaks of a time in heaven when God will judge us for our obedience to His purposes and we will be rewarded accordingly (Romans 14:10–12; 2 Corinthians 5:10).

In the Sermon on the Mount, Jesus taught about the importance of laying up "treasures in heaven" (Matthew 6:20). God has rewards in heaven for giving alms (Matthew 6:4), for prayer (Matthew 6:6), for fasting (Matthew 6:18), and even for being "persecuted for righteousness' sake" (Matthew 5:10). The Bible also speaks of special crowns in heaven: an "imperishable crown" for running God's race (1 Corinthians 9:24–27), a "crown of rejoicing" for seeing those we've won to Christ in heaven (1 Thessalonians 2:19–20), a "crown of righteousness" for obedience (2 Timothy 4:7–8), a "crown of glory" for shepherding God's people (1 Peter 5:1–4), and "the crown of life" for Christian martyrdom (Revelation 2:10). And someday, in heaven, there will be a time of casting down crowns as an ultimate act of worship before the throne of God (Revelation 4:9–11).

As we stand before our almighty, holy, and awesome Lord, we will be totally aware of the fact that our self-efforts are nothing but filthy rags (see Isaiah 64:6). Any self-made "crowns" of human efforts in missions or ministry—achieved with wrong motivations, with selfish ambitions, with family or spiritual priorities out of whack, or perhaps accomplished through direct disobedience—will be worth absolutely nothing in God's sight.

I have pictured myself entering heaven with some of these self-made crowns. As I see myself entering the awesome presence of God, all of my own crowns or achievements instantly disintegrate and evaporate into nothing.

God sees our hearts, and He can't be fooled. He sees the big picture, and He wants what's best for the long term. God has a big heart for the whole world; but He also desires a deep and personal relationship with each one of us. God wants our families to reach individuals and to touch nations; but He also wants us to reflect His love and His compassion to the people within our own home.

A mission-minded family keeps God's focus in mind. A powerful dynamic is present when you raise your children to walk daily in the fear of the Lord. It's not about preparing kids to be successful, or to get into a good college, or to make a lot of money to give to missions, or even to do something "famous" for God. Our mission is to love and please God—to live every day in complete obedience.

How this plays out for each mission-minded family will be different. God has unique purposes and callings. But we begin with the end in mind. As we're raising each of our children—from cuddling our babies, to disciplining our toddlers, to teaching and training our school-age children, to encouraging and motivating our teens, to aiming and releasing our young adults to God's call for their lives—we keep the target in focus.

It's all about worshiping God and living our lives for His glory. What we "accomplish" on earth is only a byproduct. As we draw close to God—individually and as a family unit—we will know more of His heart. We will want to follow Him. It's not about works or achievement. It's simply about loving God and doing what He wants. No matter the cost. No matter what.

For us, the "end" that we need to be concerned about is that moment when we enter heaven and appear before the presence of God. Our lives on earth are merely the preparation for our eternal life, which will continue forever. When a family lives with this focus, the dynamic is powerful. You become a family on a mission. And it's not even your own mission; you're on *God's* mission.

Dynamic #2
A Mission-Minded Family Lives in SUB-mission

A mission-minded family is submitted. There's a total submission to God and to His purposes. In archery, the arrow doesn't choose its destination; it simply rests in the archer's hand to be aimed toward his chosen target. When the archer is ready, the arrow will be released; and as long as the arrow is properly aligned and unhindered by outside forces, it will soar forward (on a straight path) toward its appointed destiny.

How SUB-mission Relates to Missions

The only difference between *submission* and *mission* is that little prefix *sub*—which means "under, beneath, or below." As mission-minded families, our daily submission to God, and our yielding to His under-the-surface guidance and His pruning in our lives, will directly affect our overall mission fulfillment and fruitfulness. It may sound more important to board an overseas-bound 747 or to have the opportunity to influence a huge crowd of people, but these activities may not be God's best plan for this particular moment (or season) in our lives.

We're all called, as believers, to be a part of God's worldwide plan; but His expectations for us, as individuals and as a family, may be much smaller, yet possibly even more challenging to obey. Today's mission-for-the-moment simply may be to open our Bible and read a few chapters or to take a minute to pray for a friend. Maybe right now all God wants is for us to snuggle up on the couch with a little one and read a fun storybook. Or perhaps God's perfect will is merely for us to quit procrastinating, turn off the computer, and go finish those loads of laundry!

When I think about the word *submission*, I like to imagine a submarine advancing silently underwater. Without sonar detection, others may not even know it's there, because it's so far beneath the surface; yet steadily and powerfully that vessel is still moving toward its goal.

Or when I think about my need to submit to God, I sometimes picture a late-winter scene with newly pruned fruit trees. Our family lives in a beautiful area of Oregon, known for its pear and apple harvests. After years of driving through the orchards, I've come to appreciate how God's fruitfulness comes in seasons. Even when the branches look barren, I know that the tree roots are growing deeper. And if I see the local farmers doing some heavy-duty pruning, I know it's only because they want an increase in their summertime harvest!

In the same way, as we establish godly and submissive hearts, we can keep advancing forward (like that underwater submarine) and growing deeper and firmer roots (like those fruit trees) to fulfill God's purposes for our lives. Even if no one notices the little things we do or the little attitudes we change, God knows it all. He knows exactly where we are right now and exactly where He's planted us. And He has not forgotten about us, or our dreams.

Submission to God involves every area of our lives: our personal maturity (spiritually, mentally, physically, and financially), our attitude toward our marriage, our family priorities, our disciplines in home management—along with our ministry callings. As we allow God to refine those *sub* areas in our lives, we can trust that He will fulfill all of His mission promises to us . . . in His timing.

SUB-mission and the Joyful Family

When God created the family, He decided upon a family structure that He knew would work best. His plan is:

- God is the leader of the family, and God's Word is the ultimate, final word.

- Dad submits to God and leads the family according to God's direction, not necessarily because he is most qualified or deserving, but because he is God's choice. Dad loves Mom with a self-sacrificing love like Christ loved the church.

- Mom submits to God and has a willing heart of submission toward her husband. Mom supports and loves Dad with a heart attitude of admiration, respect, esteem, and encouragement.

- Together, Dad and Mom seek God and God's will for their family. They diligently train each child to follow them—as they follow God.

- Each child submits completely to God and to Dad and Mom with a heart of obedience, honor, and respect. Older children are a godly example and an encouragement to younger children.

- God's purpose for this family (and for each family member) is fulfilled. The whole family loves God, and the family lives in joy.

We can't always change the actions or attitudes of others in our family, and it's not our responsibility to make sure that the people in authority over us are doing everything right. We just need to submit and obey what God is telling us.

SMUGGLING BIBLES INTO CHINA

My Personal Story of SUB-mission

Jon and I were overseas on one of our first mission trips. I was a young and adventurous twenty-two-year-old, recently graduated from college, pretty much still a newlywed, and a fairly new mommy (with a toddler in hand and baby number two on the way). Both Jon and I felt "full of faith," and we were ready to do anything for God. We had been preaching throughout remote Filipino villages and sharing in Hong Kong church services for several weeks. And on this particular morning we were preparing to smuggle Bibles (for the second time) into Communist China.

Only one week earlier, we had loaded our suitcases with Bibles and fearlessly transported God's Word through the Chinese customs department. On that first attempt our blond-haired toddler totally distracted the security guards, and no one even checked our bags! It was like we were living our very own missionary adventure; and just like the stories of Brother Andrew smuggling Bibles behind the Iron Curtain, God was once again "blinding the eyes" of foreign officials. Although we were directly disobeying a man-made law, we were totally confident in our radical obedience to God's higher law. We knew that God was blessing our actions, and we were excited to deliver His Word to believers who so desperately needed it.

However, on the morning before our second Bible-smuggling mission, my husband woke up with a feeling of apprehension in his spirit. It wasn't that Jon was fearful of what we planned to do; but he just didn't feel a peace about me going. Although he didn't know why, Jon simply felt I was not to participate in that day's outreach. Instead, he felt I was supposed to stay back and pray.

But, to put it mildly, my strong-willed, goal-oriented nature didn't quite agree with my husband's simple idea.

"You have got to be kidding!" I protested. "Do you really think I'm going to just sit here in this little room all day while you're off on our mission? I know you think I'm pushing myself too hard, but I am not too tired, and just because I'm pregnant doesn't mean I shouldn't go! I'm just fine, and I'm not going to miss out! You know, God didn't tell just *you* to 'Go into all the world and preach the gospel'; and I'm not going to sit here doing nothing! No matter what you say, I am going!"

Just like before, I felt justified in my radical obedience to God. Despite my seemingly defiant attitude, I felt totally submitted to God and His Word. (Wasn't I?) And I was steadfastly determined to fulfill God's mission.

I still had a lot to learn.

Later that morning, at our predelivery meeting place, I crammed my bags totally full of Bibles—completely assured that God would once again "blind the eyes" of anyone who would oppose us. Jon and I were assigned to cross the border at the same time as two other American pastors. As we all advanced toward the border, we hooked our little "blond-haired distraction device" into the baby-pack on Jon's back.

As the five of us came to the customs area, the two pastors decided to go through first . . . and just as we had prayed, there was no problem. Next, Jon and our son went through their line . . . and once again, there was no problem. It was as if the bags were completely invisible.

So with total assurance, I stepped forward and approached the customs desk. But suddenly a guard grabbed my heavy bag and began to unzip it. He pointed to my stacks of Bibles and began yelling in Chinese. A flashing red light began spinning above my aisle as more guards came toward me. Security guards halted Jon at the exit door, and then they ushered us into a stark room with brick walls and mean-looking officials. I tried to hold my composure and appear brave, as an English-speaking guard was called in to interpret; but as they began to yell, my wall of confidence began to crumble.

Because of our citizenship (and current international relations), the officials merely threatened us and confiscated all of our Bibles. Afterward, we were released to enter the country . . . with our empty bags. At this point, we were scheduled to go to a secret underground meeting room, where our Bibles could be sorted and organized for distribution. But now, what were we supposed to do? Together, Jon and I walked in silence for several blocks, as we tried to distance ourselves from the two pastors.

I felt so miserable, there was no need for an "I told you so." I realized that I had not just gone against my husband; I defied God and I rejected God's authority and covering over my life. Because of my stubbornness, God's protection had been removed. Instead of just doing something "little" (staying back and interceding for the group), I stubbornly pushed for my own big plan—hindering the entire mission and endangering our family.

We finally sat down, and I openly repented to Jon and the Lord. We decided to browse through an open market and eventually purchased a Chinese vase for our living room. For twenty years this vase has reminded me of how I felt that day and how deeply I want to follow God's way rather than my own.

"It is better to obey God rather than men."

BROTHER ANDREW

WHO IS BROTHER ANDREW?

Brother Andrew is known as "God's Smuggler" for his Bible distribution through a ministry called Open Doors. For years, this mission outreach has focused on areas where open propagation of Christianity is forbidden— often defying government laws and authorities to fulfill God's Great Commission. As Andrew explains, "It is better to obey God rather than men." Smuggling Bibles into "closed" countries is only one facet of Open Doors' ministry, though it's the most widely known (especially as a result of Brother Andrew's impacting book, *God's Smuggler*). This type of "illegal" ministry has stirred both controversy and tremendous support. Yet despite opposition, millions of people have received God's Word, and multitudes of people have come to know Jesus Christ as their Lord and Savior.

Dynamic #3
A Mission-Minded Family Is Strategically Aimed

Each person in your family has specific gifts and callings, and you also have a destiny as a family. God has placed you together as a powerful mission-minded unit, so it is important to seek the Lord for His purpose for you as a team.

- Is your family called to hospitality?

- Is your family called to active leadership within your local church?

- Is your family called to specifically impact your neighborhood?

- Taking into account your family's specific gifts, abilities, and resources, what are ways you can participate in God's Great Commission?

With an inward determination, the archer reaches across his shoulder and selects a favorite arrow. He checks the alignment, then places it in his bow. With his eye focused on the target's center, he gently pulls back, feeling the string tighten and the tension increase.

Our children are God's reward and our heritage. Our descendants have the potential to take God's mission into future generations—and to a higher and more effective level. They're our arrows, our most strategic weapons to aim toward the future.

Our goal is not to raise kids to be popular, famous, or wealthy. The goal is not to somehow get our teenagers to "survive" their youth without tasting a drop of alcohol, puffing on a cigarette, or experimenting with illegal drugs. It's not enough to "hope" that each child will turn out OK or "trust" that they won't be "too bad." As we influence tomorrow's world changers, our vision must be infinitely higher.

Can you imagine an archer distracted by his surroundings and pledging, "OK, in today's competition I'll try not to hit that tree, and I won't shoot any arrows into the river; I'll work at aiming higher than the grass and try not to skewer my opponent"?

This contestant will likely miss even the outer rings of his target!

Instead of focusing on the "NO" side of human legalism (emphasizing our never-ending rules), it's much more fulfilling and productive to challenge young people to live on the "YES" side of God's life (emphasizing His eternal plans).

For example, if a daughter keeps focused on her desire to have a happy family with a godly, mission-minded husband, she will be self-motivated to make pure and wholesome relationship decisions throughout her childhood and young adult years.

If a son is attentive to a specific calling on his life toward a particular ministry, he will realize the importance of developing his personal prayer life, he will want to faithfully study the Bible, and, in God's timing, he will begin to step out in areas of Christian leadership.

As we keep each of our children focused on God's long-term goals, today's short-term decisions will make sense. And today's temptations, by God's grace, will be easier to withstand. Why would our kids want to smoke or take drugs? They'll want to set nations "on fire" for God! Why would our teens seek satisfaction in ungodly relationships? Their hearts will be burning with the fear of God and will be focused on His passion for the lost! (And if that attitude is not a reality in our kids' lives today, let's pray for it—in faith!)

Proverbs 22:6 tells us, according to *The Amplified Bible*, "Train up a child in the way he should go [and in keeping with his individual gift or bent], and when he is old he will not depart from it." This instruction goes beyond training a child merely to "believe" in God. Our responsibility as mission-minded parents is to train each child to "know" Jesus personally, to hear His voice, and to follow God's direction for his or her life.

As you consider each family member, and your family as a unit, several questions can help you "aim" toward God's mission-minded purpose:

- What is each family member's unique talent, gift, or personality strength?

- What does each family member love to do?

- What is each family member passionate about? (Conversely, what causes him or her to get extremely frustrated?)

- What could be one of God's purposes for each person?

- As a family, how can we make the best use of the childhood and teenage years for the kingdom of God—both for the present and for the future?

With his eye focused on the target, the archer pauses a moment. He relaxes ever so slightly . . . then prepares his arrow. He points it toward the bull's-eye and makes certain the aim is correct. Then, at last, he releases the string.

As our children grow, increasingly we will need to challenge them to step out and try new things (in a good way). If a child is trained and disciplined properly during the younger years, the older years will not be a time for our gripping harder, but for relaxing our "hold" to begin letting go. The teen years are a time to practice aiming our arrows. Especially during the middle school and high school years, it is important to encourage our children to take godly risks, to discover God's desires, and to work with them to develop every area of life:

- **Spiritual Development**—The core of our mission-minded foundation is each family member's personal relationship with Jesus. If this goal is not in place, nothing will line up. Each child can be challenged to read through the Bible, to pray for the nations, and to step out in leadership. Perhaps a child could assist with a children's Bible study or become a prayer leader. Perhaps a teenager could help lead a youth worship team or go on an adventurous mission trip.

- **Mental Development**—Educationally, think about God's purpose for your family and for each of your children. Will God's calling require a university degree, advanced mathematics or science, writing skills, or knowledge of computer technology? How should that affect your family's attitude toward education? Is your family gifted in music or art? That talent should be developed and focused toward God's kingdom. If future finances for college will be a challenge, begin researching scholarships (and encourage your kids in areas these scholarships evaluate, such as GPA, test scores, community service hours, and leadership).

- **Physical Development**—A mission-minded family is active and physically fit. The childhood years are important for developing a wholesome lifestyle, and an adventurous attitude can be encouraged. God's life purpose may require strong physical abilities or a daring mindset. Perhaps your family should invest time in athletic training, competing on a local sports team, simply working on losing excess weight, or changing unhealthy eating habits. Physical fitness is not merely for appearance and the thrill of competition; it's vital for health, self-discipline, and becoming more goal oriented.

As mission-minded families, we can seek God's direction and then begin to serve as God's facilitators and motivators. If we can encourage our children to discover God's plans and to *want to* develop specific God-given abilities, it will totally change everything. Instead of dealing with surface issues, we begin to train our children's hearts and to focus on staying aimed toward God's purpose. A change at this root level alters everything, from grades in school and success in activities to confidence in leadership and a spiritual desire to develop God-glorifying friendships.

— 👫 FROM MY CHILDREN'S PERSPECTIVE —

MISSION-MINDED LEADERSHIP

By Christi Dunagan, age seventeen

As I've grown up in leadership and as I've grown into increased responsibilities, I've learned that leadership from God's standpoint is not a part-time activity. Leadership requires living a continuous and "real" lifestyle that others can follow, whether "leading" a specific activity or not.

A godly leader can't just *talk* about how to do things; instead, he or she needs to *walk* it out. That means setting a positive example and "guarding the gates" of life—the eye gate (including what movies I watch and what I read), the ear gate (including what music I listen to and who I talk to), and the mouth gate (what I say). I realize it is very important to stand firm in my beliefs, moral standards, and convictions, even when it's tough, because I never want to cause anyone to stumble or fall.

One thing my family has taught me about mission-minded leadership is that a "big" aspect of leadership is being "small" enough to be a servant. As a leader, it's not that we're "more important"; we're simply willing to sacrifice our time, energy, and emotions to concern ourselves with others. We must look beyond our own needs to help make a difference in the lives of others. We need to put other people's needs ahead of our own and keep the best interests of others in mind. As a leader, it's not that we're "above" other people; but we need to live "above the norm," with a higher standard—which often simply means working harder, being willing to be different, and not being afraid to walk alone.

So how do you reach God's destiny for your family? Practically speaking, it's as simple as the sport of archery. Point A is the tip of the arrow (where you are today). Point B is the center of the bull's-eye (where God wants you to go and what He wants you to do). God is the Archer, and our part is simply to allow Him to aim us—on a straight line—toward His purpose.

As individuals, and as a family unit, we allow God to use the gifts He has given us to fulfill His plans for our lives. We realize that each child is God's special arrow; therefore, as parents we help to keep each one polished, aligned, and aimed toward his or her destiny. As mission-minded families, we train and prepare "on target" with God's plans.

Walking to the target, the archer gives a faint smile. He pauses to admire how fine his arrow looks in the center of that red circle. Finally, he gives a slight tug, polishes his arrow, and then places it back in his quiver. Today's shot was only practice; but someday, when it's time for a real battle, he knows this arrow will hit its mark.

THE CALL FOR REAPERS

A missions hymn, by John O. Thompson (1782–1818)

Far and near the fields are teeming
With the waves of ripened grain;
Far and near their gold is gleaming
O'er the sunny slope and plain.

Send them forth with morn's first beaming;
Send them in the noontide's glare;
When the sun's last rays are gleaming,
Bid them gather ev'rywhere.

O thou, whom thy Lord is sending,
Gather now the sheaves of gold;
Heav'nward then at evening wending,
Thou shalt come with joy untold.

Chorus:
Lord of harvest, send for reapers!
Hear us, Lord, to Thee we cry;
Send them now the sheaves to gather,
Ere the harvesttime pass by.

"The supreme task of the church is the
evangelization of the world."

"Untold millions are still untold."

"You have one business on earth—to save souls."

JOHN WESLEY

Part II

Our Godly Tug of War: Balancing Our Passions

CHAPTER 3

Divine Tension for
Our Family Bow

Jesus asks us, "What will it profit a man if he gains the whole world, and loses his own soul?" (Mark 8:36). I also wonder what it will profit a mission-minded family to lead multitudes of unreached people to Christ . . . and lose even one of its own kids.

We need to balance our outward calling to others with our inward calling to love God and our own family. We need to balance our desire to "do" something for God with His calling for us simply to "know" Him. Yes, we need to love and reach the world; but we also need to love those God has placed in our closest circle of influence.

THE PRAYING MOMMAS AND THE SCREAMING BABIES

About five thousand women gathered for a week of ministry, teaching, and worship. The accommodations for our African village conference were humble. Bamboo awnings covered with tarps provided shade from the hot sun, and most of the women simply brought straw mats for sleeping. Many women also brought little children and nursing babies, whom they cared for as they listened to the sessions. One morning I got up and took an early morning prayer-walk, and I was blessed (and challenged) to see hundreds of women gathered for a time of fervent prayer.

As I walked quietly behind the group, I noticed a few women who were praying very hard and loud, but then I noticed that these women were totally oblivious to the needs of their little babies—sitting with bare bottoms in wet little puddles in the dirt, screaming at the top of their lungs. As I watched for a few moments, I wondered what God thought about their fervent prayers. One by one I picked up the babies and tried to help them stop crying, handing each one to his or her momma.

Later that day I shared with the women about the importance of balancing our ministry with our family priorities. Yet I was also challenged on a personal level. How many times does God see my own out-of-balance efforts, like when I'm at work on the computer or busy with a mission project—and my little kids are plopped down in front of one-too-many videos? I want God to hear my prayers, and I want my efforts to be actions of obedience. I need to keep balanced.

God wants Christian marriages to be reflections of Christ's love, and He wants each parent-child relationship to be a reflection of the heavenly Father's care. There will be times of sacrifice, of course, but our families shouldn't be neglected because of our mission-minded commitment.

Coming to Terms with Our Missionary Heritage

The other day I received a thought-provoking e-mail from a new college graduate who recently became acquainted with our family. "I have always had an issue with the family/missions life." This young man explained, "I could never fix those two together in my head. But now I know there is plenty of hope to have the large family I've always wanted (Bless my wife!) and being in full-time missions."

The more I've thought about this comment, the more I've realized how hard it is to find solid examples of world-impacting missionaries who also had strong family priorities. We can't deny that complete obedience to God's call requires sacrifice. There may be occasions of separation, financial challenge, or even death. It's possible that a family member could step out in perfect obedience—and contract some tropical illness, or be martyred, or die in an accident. In fact, instead of just "blowing off" those missionaries who didn't keep their priorities in order, we need to realize that many great men and women of God earnestly sought God for answers. International travel was very difficult in days past, and missionary work was dangerous. But if the missionary pioneers wouldn't have made these sacrifices, who knows where the worldwide church would be today?

One example is Jonathan (1859–1936) and Rosalind (1864–1942) Goforth and their eleven children. This tremendous Canadian missionary family brought the gospel to China in the early years of the twentieth century. Their passion for the lost resulted in multitudes coming to Christ, often through creative ways of evangelism. One year their family invited over twenty-five thousand people (all curious to learn how foreigners lived) to tour their house; as small groups came through their home, Jonathan preached the gospel (up to eight hours a day) while Rosalind and the children served tea and visited with the women. They traveled as a family to many villages throughout China, staying in an area until a national evangelist and a new church could be established. But it wasn't always easy. Five children died in childhood, and there were excruciating times of family separation. The following excerpt is especially thought provoking.

THE DIFFICULT DILEMMA OF JONATHAN GOFORTH

An excerpt from Goforth of China,
by Rosalind Goforth

While Rosalind fully supported her husband's dedication to the Lord, she was naturally concerned at times about his dedication to her and the children. Of course God's will was paramount, but must it be at odds with what was in the best interest of the family? As a wife, she never doubted his love, but she did on occasion feel less than fully secure in her position. Before she and the children returned to Canada alone in 1908, she probed him concerning his commitment to her: "Suppose I were stricken with an incurable disease in the homeland and had but a few months to live. If we cabled you to come, would you come?"

Goforth obviously did not want to answer the question. An outright "no" would have been too harsh, but Rosalind persisted until he gave his answer—in the form of a question to her: "Suppose our country were at war with another nation and I, a British officer in command of an important unit. Much depended upon me as commander as to whether it was to be victory or defeat. Would I, in that event, be permitted to forsake my post in response to a call from my family in the homeland, even if it were what you suggest?" What could she say? She had no choice but to sadly reply, "No."

When my husband and I dedicated our lives to full-time missions over twenty years ago, we committed ourselves to a ministry characterized by a strong marriage. In our view, raising and training our seven children is not a distraction to our mission calling; it is our primary ministry! And today, as our children grow and pursue God's call on their lives, our family's mission-minded impact is multiplying!

There will be times of laying down our lives and taking up our cross, but we need to live in the power of the resurrection. One of my favorite quotes comes from George MacDonald: "We die daily. Happy those who daily come to life as well." That theme is similar to Paul's words, "I have been crucified with Christ; it is no longer I who live, but Christ lives in me" (Galatians 2:20). God has called us to live and to share His abundant life! Our marriages, and our families, and each of our children should benefit from our walk with God—in a way that non-Christians would envy.

As mission-minded families, how can we balance our passion for missions with our heart for our home? Is it possible to make a significant world impact while maintaining God's peace and joy in our own families? Do we have to choose between "raising our kids" and "reaching the lost"—or is it possible to do both?

I believe that God always has a perfect balance for these two pursuits; yet His guidance for one family is not necessarily the same as His guidance for another. Even within our individual lives, God's direction for today may be different from His direction for tomorrow. The important thing is that each of us, as parents and as servants of Jesus Christ, must come to God day by day and simply obey what He tells us to do!

Every Family Needs This Balance!

This godly tug of war—between our passions for our family and for missions—doesn't just affect full-time missionaries. Perhaps a little one tugs at a mother's legs as she's in the middle of a desperate phone call from a friend who needs prayer. Perhaps a dad feels overloaded with responsibilities at church, but God urges his heart to take time to nurture his own marriage. What about times when you're so busy reaching out for God that you don't take time for God to reach out to you?

If you're passionate about missions *and* passionate about your family, there will be times when this godly tug of war will seem intense, with both sides pulling hard. Have you ever sat in a mission-focused worship service and listened to a compelling message about the plight of the lost or the urgent need for world evangelization . . . and then looked at those precious children sitting next to you and prayed, *Lord, how can I possibly respond to this urgency I'm feeling in my spirit? I desperately want Your heart for the lost and for the nations, but I also know that You've called me to raise and train my kids! What am I supposed to do?*

As the preacher finishes his heart-wrenching sermon, have you ever tried to balance your inward dreams with your current reality? Have you ever longed to do something BIG for God, while knowing that He does see (and smile at) every little thing you do? Have you ever felt an inward tug of war in which your heart desperately longs to do more for missions, yet you want to be obedient by maintaining a deep and real contentment by doing less (especially if nothing you are doing at the moment feels very "significant" for God's kingdom)?

I know I sure have!

But I believe these two pulls can be a godly struggle. We need to keep pressing in toward God to get more of His heart and His love for the world; and at the same time we need to keep moving forward, little by little, to help raise up a new generation for Jesus. By keeping these two callings in balance, our families (and our ministries, and even our children's future ministries, in God's timing) will powerfully radiate His love!

It is true that being a godly parent is a mission in and of itself, yet we cannot forget that Jesus died for more people than the few precious individuals who sit around our dining table! God's love reaches beyond our homes, beyond our churches, and beyond our local areas. God sees from a different dimension than we do. His perspective is from eternity, and His vantage point is from heaven. As He views every decision we make, He sees His entire universe! So if we want our decisions to line up with His will, we need to seek the truth from God's unchanging Word, be willing to see the needs of this world, and seek God's perfect wisdom through prayer!

God's heart is for His kingdom and for the world . . . and He needs our families to be strong. As mission-minded families, living with these two seemingly opposing passions can sometimes seem like a delicate balance. But perhaps, if we keep this bowstring tight, with both sides pulling intensely and in balance, our family's arrows will shoot farther and more accurately than ever.

DIVINE ORDER FOR EACH DAY

An excerpt from *Extravagant Worship*, by Darlene Zschech

For years, I tried to juggle all the elements of life. I knew there was a God call on my life to be in ministry, and yet I also knew that it could never be at the expense of my family. When I tried to juggle all the boxes,

I learned the hard way that it is difficult to keep them all from crashing down. So I no longer have boxes for marriage, ministry, and motherhood. Instead, God has shown me that there is a divine order for my life.

Instead of trying to make sure that everything is balanced (there is no prescribed formula of balance), God showed me that I am to break out of the box mentality and instead seek Him for divine order for my life. Each day differs from the day before. The dynamics change, but the call on my life doesn't. Marriage, motherhood, and ministry are all cohesively part of that call. God anoints us for our entire call.

WHO IS DARLENE ZSCHECH?

Darlene Zschech is a worship leader and a world-impacting minister from Sydney, Australia. Her passion is leading people into the presence of God and seeing them realize their full potential in Him. Darlene has written over seventy worship songs, including "Shout to the Lord," a beautiful chorus sung by millions of churchgoers. Many of her songs emphasize the importance of reaching the lost: "You Are My World," "Call Upon His Name," "Touching Heaven, Changing Earth," and "Change Your World."

Darlene and her husband, Mark, serve as a vital part of the leadership team of their church; and Darlene leads worship most weeks for a television program, which reaches over 180 countries around the globe. She also ministers through teaching, writing, supporting her husband, and being a loving mother to their three children.

Finding the Divine Tension

Two strong pulls are required for powerful divine tension in a mission-minded family. First, there needs to be a fervent heart for the family (inwardly founded on a personal relationship *with* Jesus); and second, there needs to be a fire to fulfill God's purpose (outwardly focused on reaching others *for* Jesus).

Such a family is like a mighty bow with a string securely fastened on both ends. It doesn't just have a flippantly tied strand that is "well-balanced," but it has a heavy-duty line with a divine tension that is strong, tight, and powerful!

FAREWELL TO THE BALANCED LIFE

An excerpt from *The Missions Addiction*, by David Shibley

The normal Christian life is anything but balanced, as popularly defined. . . . The normal Christian life is high risk and high joy. The normal Christian life releases the temporal to embrace the eternal. It is a life lived in the love of God.

It is normal for us to be passionate about what God is passionate about! . . . This is not a call to discard balance, but rather to redefine it. Yes, there is a rhythm of life, and long-term effectiveness mandates that, like our Lord, we have seasons when we "come aside . . . and rest a while" (Mark 6:31). It's OK to stop and smell the roses. But the flip side of that coin is there is also a time to "spend and be spent" for the gospel.

God is not calling us to win the world and, in the process, lose our families. But I have known those who so enshrined family life and were so protective of "quality time" that the children never saw in their parents the kind of consuming love that made their *parents'* faith attractive to them. Some have lost their children, not because they weren't at their soccer games or didn't take family vacations, but because they never transmitted a loyalty to Jesus that went deep enough to interrupt personal preferences.

I want my family to have that kind of consuming love, with high risk and high joy. I want to live out my faith in a way that is not only attractive but also compelling and irresistible! I want to be moved by the passions of God's heart—and for my kids to take these godly passions to a deeper level. I want to hand off the baton to my descendants and have them run faster and farther than I ever did. I want my kids to impact their generation with a greater boldness, wisdom, and effectiveness than I ever have. Why? Because God's Word tells us, "Of the increase of His government and peace, there will be no end" (Isaiah 9:7). As Christians, we should always be moving in the right direction. Or as the famous missionary evangelist David Livingstone once said, he was willing "to go anywhere, provided it be forward."

May each of our arrows be aimed with exact precision, with just the right "divine tension" on our family's bowstring, so that every arrow released will pierce God's intended bull's-eye. May each of our arrows do damage to the enemy's cause and make a strategic difference for the kingdom of God.

CHAPTER 4

Missionary Heroes
and Their Families

Many missionaries have accomplished great things for God. Some have been courageous single men (such as Patrick, Francis Xavier, and "Bruchko" Olson) or daring single women (such as Amy Carmichael, Lottie Moon, and Rachel Saint). But many missionary heroes have had families, with spouses to care for and children to train.

It is interesting to consider the families of renowned missionaries, looking at how they balanced the dual responsibilities of their ministries to others and their duties at home. Unfortunately, it doesn't take long to realize that many missionary heroes *with* families were not heroes *of* the family. A few of the "biggest" names in missions history (such as William Carey, David Livingstone, and C. T. Studd) had severe family problems; yet others (such as William and Catherine Booth, Hudson and Maria Taylor, and George and Mary Müller) found a powerful and harmonious ministry-family balance.

When God commissions a person for a ministry assignment, He sees the whole picture. Yes, God wants His mission accomplished; but He also wants that person to remain steadfast in relationship with Him and to leave a godly and lasting legacy. With a divinely ordered life, a person's family *and* ministry can be fruitful and full of joy. If these two "pulls" are balanced, a person's ministry can be *more* effective; and when that individual's life is over, his or her descendants can continue (with similar passions and convictions) to expand God's kingdom into the next generation.

🔔 TEACHING OPPORTUNITY

Mini Mission Biographies and
Mission-Minded Monologue Skits

This chapter includes mini-biographies of many prominent missionary heroes, with an emphasis on couples and families. These brief summaries can serve as a quick missionary reference guide. Included are recommendations for great family-friendly resources (to help introduce you and your children to the lives of these men and women of God), classic missions excerpts, and seven informative "mission-minded monologue skits" for a member of your family, or someone else, to perform.

An Old Testament Missionary Hero:
FATHER ABRAHAM

The calling of a patriarch and his family

Family-Friendly Resources:

• The biblical account in Genesis 12–18

• Read the story of God's covenant with Abraham from several Bible storybooks, and compare the vision for reaching the nations with the Genesis account.

In many missions-training programs, God's covenant with Abraham is emphasized, showing God's heart for all people and how Abraham and his family were blessed (God's "top-line" blessing) to be a blessing to the nations (God's "bottom-line" blessing): "In you all the families of the earth shall be blessed" (Genesis 12:3). Abraham left his father's land to go to an unknown land; he interceded for two wicked cities; and he was chosen because God knew that he would train his children.

The LORD said, "Shall I hide from Abraham what I am doing, since Abraham shall surely become a great and mighty nation, and all the nations of the earth shall be blessed in him? For I have known him, in order that he may command his children and his household after him, that they keep the way of the LORD, to do righteousness and justice, that the LORD may bring to Abraham what He has spoken to him." (Genesis 18:17–19)

A New Testament Missionary Hero: PHILIP THE EVANGELIST

A faithful servant, with a mission-minded family

Family-Friendly Resources:

- The biblical accounts in Acts 6, 8, and 21

- Mission-Minded Monologue Skit (below)

Mission-Minded Monologue Skit #1

Costume: *Have Philip wear a Bible-time robe*

Setting: *Inside Philip's home; include a few simple props, such as a mat, table, or basin*

PHILIP: Welcome to my home! I am the only one here now, since my wife is gone and our four daughters are with some of our Christian friends who live near the synagogue. And *Who am I?* you might ask. My name is Philip, and I am an evangelist. I live here . . . in the city of Caesarea . . . on the coast of the Mediterranean Sea, although I have traveled to many different places to share the Good News of my Lord Jesus Christ.

My ministry actually began quite humbly, since the apostles in Jerusalem needed some help to care for the widows. These church leaders were looking for "men of good reputation, full of the Holy Spirit and wisdom"; and I was one of the seven brothers chosen. I know how important it is to have a servant's heart, so I was willing to do whatever needed to be done. Then the seven of us rejoiced as the word of God spread and the number of disciples multiplied greatly.

Some time later our church in Jerusalem began to suffer persecution, so I went to Samaria. There I had the opportunity to preach the gospel, and multitudes came to Christ—with mighty miracles, deliverances, and healings. But then, right in the middle of all that citywide excitement, an angel of God spoke to me with a word of direction. The Lord wanted me to leave and go to a specific road out in the middle of a desert! It didn't make sense, but I obeyed.

As I was alone in that wilderness . . . I waited for a while . . . and wondered why God had called me to that barren place.

But then I noticed a chariot in the distance, and the Holy Spirit spoke to me and told me to go up to this chariot. Immediately I ran and caught up with the chariot, and I met a high-ranking governmental official from Ethiopia. This important African man was sitting in his chariot reading from the Book of Isaiah, but he couldn't understand what the Scripture passage meant. God helped me as I began with the passage in Isaiah and told the man about Jesus.

It was a powerful time of sharing the gospel. The official gave his life to Christ and immediately wanted to be baptized—in some water alongside of the road! Then, before I could even begin any "salvation follow-up procedures," something miraculous happened. God instantly transported me—or "zapped" me—to the city of Azotus, where I began preaching the gospel in city after city.

I love to go to different places to preach, but I also enjoy being home. Did you know that when the apostle Paul and his ministry team needed a place to stay, my family and I housed them right here in our home for many days? Hospitality is important to me. And I consider it an honor to raise my children for the Lord. I have four unmarried daughters who are known for their purity of heart and as young women who prophesy, or speak forth God's word, by the power of the Holy Spirit.

My children deeply love God and are sensitive to the Spirit's leading. Together, as we follow our Lord Jesus Christ, we have a family ministry. We want to obey whatever God tells us to do (whether big or small), and our home life is in order. People call me "Philip the evangelist"; but I see myself as God's humble servant . . . with a family that simply loves Jesus.

An Early Church Martyr: PERPETUA

A single mother who put God first

Family-Friendly Resources:

- The Voice of the Martyrs website (www.persecution.com), which has many excellent resources for children and families pertaining to persecuted believers.

- Mission-Minded Monologue Skit (below)

Mission-Minded Monologue Skit #2

Costume: *A middle-aged woman richly dressed in an elegant gown*

Setting: *A wealthy home during the third century; for effect, add a white pillar, a stone bench, plants in stonelike pottery, or a trellis*

PERPETUA'S MOTHER: It has been over two hundred years since that Jewish teacher Jesus was crucified. Yet His life still affects the whole Roman Empire. Here, in the city of Carthage, in North Africa, my husband is a respected and wealthy nobleman. I want to tell you about our twenty-two-year-old daughter, Perpetua. Our leaders were persecuting followers of this Jesus; yet, despite this risk, our daughter decided to join them.

Perpetua hadn't been married long when she lost her husband. So she was responsible, as a single mother, for her little baby, my grandson. And she was also following that dangerous group of Jesus followers, called "Christians."

My husband and I were so worried for Perpetua, and then our greatest fears were realized as she was thrown into prison because of her beliefs. My husband even went to visit her in that terrible cell in an attempt to convince her to reject her newfound faith. He begged our daughter to put family considerations above her creed, but Perpetua refused to turn from her faith in Jesus. She was genuinely grieved about the pain she caused her father and me, especially as she entrusted her little son into the care of her brother and me. As she handed me her baby, I knew that she deeply loved her child; yet it was evident that she was even more concerned about her loyalty to Christ.

What happened next was horrifying. My daughter was sent into the arena with a wild cow, where she was tortured so brutally the crowd began to yell, "Enough!" But afterward, I heard how she comforted her Christian friends by saying, "Give out the Word to the brothers and sisters; stand fast in the faith, love one another, and don't let our suffering become a stumbling block to you." My daughter was finally beheaded by a gladiator.

Perpetua chose her Christian faith over her family's pleas that she renounce her faith to save her life—but because of her steadfastness, I now know that my daughter's faith was real.

NARRATOR: After Perpetua's death there was relative peace for nearly fifty years, and the Christian church grew. [1]

Colonial Missionaries:
JOHN AND HANNA ELIOT

"Apostle to the Indians" (1604–1690)

Family-Friendly Resource:

*   Mission-Minded Monologue Skit (below)

Mission-Minded Monologue Skit #3

Costume: Traditional "Pilgrim" or early American style dress, with knee-length dark pants, white socks, dark shoes, dark jacket, and white shirt, with a ribbon tied at the neck

Setting: The early colonial years in America; John Eliot is sitting outside, perhaps on a log, holding a small Bible opened to the Book of Psalms

JOHN ELIOT: My name is John Eliot. People often refer to me as the "Apostle to the Indians." I was born in England and educated at the famous university at Cambridge. After graduating, I met a Puritan pastor and saw in his family the life-giving power of godliness. This family led me to know Jesus Christ in a personal way. I was so moved by the experience that, in 1631, I set sail for the new land of America to become a minister myself.

A year after my arrival, my lovely fiancée, Hanna Mumford, joined me; and in October of 1632, we were married (which was the first recorded wedding in our town). For eleven years we ministered in a colonial church, but Hanna and I began to see the need to focus on reaching the Indians.* When I turned forty, I began studying a tribal language and traveling with a young interpreter.

As I led meetings for these native people, I often ministered to children and families, and many times I distributed treats following the services. I liked to drill the children in recitation of the catechism—the foundational truths of Christianity—and the parents would learn as they listened. At times, when I preached on the Ten Commandments and on Christ's love, some of the people would respond with tears and weeping. There were questions that followed—but the most difficult question to answer was "Why has no white man ever told us these things before?"

The new believers were often rejected by their families, so my wife and I set up towns of "Christian Indians." By 1671 we had gathered 1,100 believers into fourteen "praying towns." Desiring their spiritual growth, I worked hard to translate the Bible into their native language, although I was often criticized for "wasting time" with a tribal tongue when I could have been teaching them English.

Hanna and I were blessed with six children, although several died in infancy. Despite hardships, I have always believed in being positive. I love God's Word, and many consider it interesting that I published the very first book in America: a Christian book about the Psalms. [2]

* now known as Native American or First Nations people

THE GREAT REMORSE OF COUNT ZINZENDORF

Count Nicolaus Ludwig von Zinzendorf (1700–1760) founded the Moravian Church, which emphasized single-mindedness, identification with the cross, and world evangelization. In 1727, the Moravians began a prayer vigil that continued, uninterrupted, twenty-four hours a day, seven days a week, for over a hundred years. As a result of this prayer movement—combined with Moravian missionary evangelism—a tremendous revival began. The Moravians helped spread Christianity throughout the world.

Yet the success of this great movement came at great expense to family life. The Moravians emphasized that the needs of the ministry took priority over the needs of the family. Youth were challenged to accept the call of lifelong singleness; and when permitted to marry, they often had their spouse selected for them (or chosen by lot). Everything was abandoned for the sake of the cross. Wives and children were frequently left behind, since God's "mission work" took absolute priority.

The Moravians' founder, Count Zinzendorf, was a prime example of this ambitious missionary focus. His wife, Erdmuth, was a proficient assistant in regard to missionary office work; but she and the Zinzendorf children were usually left behind (once for more than ten years) as Nicolaus ministered abroad. During the last fifteen years of their marriage, the couple's affection toward each other became cold and lifeless. Yet it was not until after Erdmuth's death that Nicolaus finally realized his errors, with repentance and regret. Count Zinzendorf deeply grieved his loss—not only for the loss of his wife but also for the life together they never had.

In *Count Zinzendorf*, biographer John R. Weinlick writes, "The count's sorrow was aggravated by remorse. He had not been fair to Erdmuth. Cynics to the contrary, he had not been unfaithful during their long periods of separation; but he had been extremely thoughtless. He had forgotten that she was a woman, a wife, and a mother." [3]

WILLIAM AND DOROTHY CAREY

The "Father of Modern Missions" . . . and his sad family

William Carey is known as the "Father of Modern Missions." His motto, "Expect great things from God; attempt great things for

God!" has challenged believers for generations. He led great translation works and encouraged many Christians to become actively involved in world missions. Yet despite these achievements, a mere glance at William Carey's family life presents a sobering message. God's work should not be done at the expense of everything else. God used Carey in a mighty way; but important lessons can be learned from this famous missionary's mistakes, as well as from his victories.

William Carey had long been interested in the needs of world missions; yet when he finally decided to go to India himself, the response he received was terrible. His church was distressed about losing its pastor, and his father thought he was fanatical. Yet these oppositions were nothing compared with the outrage of Carey's wife. At the time, William and Dorothy Carey had three young children, and Mrs. Carey was pregnant with their fourth child. The proposed five-month voyage to India was extremely perilous, and Dorothy had no desire to live, and to raise their children, in that dangerous tropical land. The current political situation made the decision even more treacherous, since France had just declared war on England.

As Ruth A. Tucker explains in *From Jerusalem to Irian Jaya*, "Other women had willingly made such sacrifices and thousands more would in the future, but Dorothy was different. If there is a 'Mother of Modern Missions,' it is certainly not she. She defiantly refused to go. . . . Carey, though distressed by her decision, was determined to go, even if it meant going without her." [4]

Because of an unexpected turn of events, Carey's missionary venture was delayed; and by that time Mrs. Carey had delivered their baby (just a few weeks earlier). With much urging, and despite her grumbling, Dorothy and the children were persuaded to join the group right before the team's departure. However, the decision proved to be a disaster.

Physically, Dorothy's health was weak; emotionally, she continually complained; and mentally, she was quite disturbed. When one of their children (a five-year-old son named Peter) tragically died, all of these problems intensified; and from this point, it seems that Dorothy Carey had a complete mental breakdown. Coworkers began to refer to Mrs. Carey as "wholly deranged" and even "insane."

In John Marshman's biography of Carey, he describes the great missionary focused on his translation work, "while an insane wife, frequently wrought up to a state of most distressing excitement, was in the next room." [5]

Dorothy Carey died when she was fifty-one years old (in 1807); yet it seems as if William Carey felt more *relieved* than *grieved* by the loss. For years, she had contributed nothing to the mission work except problems and complaints.

William Carey seemed to also ignore his parenting responsibilities. Similar to the neglectful fathering of the biblical high priest Eli (who grieved over his disobedient sons but would not restrain them; see 1 Samuel 2:22 and 3:13), Carey knew that his sons were having problems, but he was unwilling to confront them.

Again, Ruth A. Tucker explains, "As busy as he was, Carey was unable to give his children the fathering they so desperately needed. Even when he was with them his easy-going nature stood in the way of firm discipline, a lack that was plainly exhibited in the boys' behavior." [6]

When a fellow missionary, Hannah Marshman, mother of Carey's biographer John Marshman, first met the Carey family in 1800, she was shocked by the way in which William Carey looked after his four sons— noting that they were undisciplined, unmannered, and even uneducated. Carey hadn't spoiled them but had simply ignored them. Hannah wrote, "The good man saw and lamented the evil but was too mild to apply an effectual remedy." [7]

Even though Carey is remembered as the "Father of Modern Missions," he was severely deficient in his commitment to "father" his own family.

American Pioneer Missionaries: MARCUS AND NARCISSA WHITMAN

Missionaries in the Oregon Territory; martyred in 1847

Family-Friendly Resources:

*   *Attack in the Rye Grass: Marcus and Narcissa Whitman* (Trailblazer Books), by Dave and Neta Jackson, Bethany House, 1994

*   Mission-Minded Monologue Skit (below)

Mission-Minded Monologue Skit #4

Costume: *Prairie-style dress and bonnet*

Setting: *A rugged outdoor area*

NARCISSA WHITMAN: Oh, isn't this area beautiful? With its towering evergreen trees, majestic waterfalls, and gorgeous mountains, this land in the northwest region of America is truly breathtaking. My name is Narcissa Whitman; and my husband, Marcus Whitman, and I are Christian missionaries here in the vast and rugged Oregon Territory.

Back when I was Narcissa Prentiss, before I was married, I heard a passionate plea made by a missionary named Samuel Parker. As he shared about the need for taking the gospel of Jesus Christ to the unreached Indians* of the West, I wanted to go—and I wanted to go alone—but the mission board would not accept me as a single woman.

Later, Marcus Whitman approached me with his own missionary ambitions, for that same missionary had influenced him. Mr. Whitman presented me with the idea of marriage, primarily as a business or ministry proposition. But naturally I had to think about it for a while.

He went ahead and traveled on a mission outreach by himself but returned home within only a few months to ask again for my hand in marriage. I decided to accept his invitation, and the day after our wedding we left for Missouri to join our missionary expedition to Oregon. A year later, when Marcus and I found out that God was blessing us with a baby, I finally realized . . . that I was in love!

Although the journey was difficult, I loved the wilderness and was overwhelmed by the beauty of God's creation. In Oregon, we settled in an area called Waiilatpu, and we began to minister to a tribe of people called the Cayuse.

Our missionary group was entirely on our own, so we became very busy building shelters and planting crops. We began to minister—trying to learn the native language, helping with medical needs, and sharing the gospel. Other missionaries came to join us, but this new "help" was actually nothing but trouble. Usually I was so busy caring for visitors and seven precious children whose parents had died on the journey that I had little time for anything else.

Just recently, the people we have been trying to reach have faced a terrible plague. Marcus and I, and our coworkers, have attempted to help them, yet the tribe thinks that our "white man's medicine" contained poison. Right now, the situation is intense. I don't know what will happen. Yet I know that God brought us here, and I believe that the message of the gospel will continue to go forward . . . no matter what.

* now known as Native American or First Nations people

NARRATOR: In 1847, five Cayuse Indians (whom the Whitmans knew well) came to the Oregon mission and massacred Marcus, Narcissa, and twelve other men. Years later, missionaries witnessed a great movement of God as hundreds of native people were converted to Christ and baptized.

The Father of American Missions: ADONIRAM JUDSON

A sad missionary family "saga"

Family-Friendly Resources:

- Wholesome Words website: "Adoniram Judson: American Baptist Missionary to Burma" (http://www. wholesomewords.org/biography/ biorpjudson.html); "Ann H. Judson: The First Lady of American Foreign Missions" (http://www.wholesomewords. org/biography/biorpannjudson.html); Children's Corner, Missionary Heroes: "The Three Mrs. Judsons" (http://www. wholesomewords.org/children/heroes/hmrsjud.html)

- "Adoniram and Ann Judson: America's First Foreign Missionaries," in *Hero Tales*, Vol. 1, by Dave and Neta Jackson, Bethany House, 2005

- *Imprisoned in the Golden City: Adoniram and Ann Judson* (Trailblazer Books), by Dave and Neta Jackson, Bethany House, 1993

Adoniram Judson (1788–1850) is known as the "Father of American Missions." He married three times during his lifetime, since twice he suffered the death of a beloved wife. Adoniram's family was often separated for extended periods, and seven of his thirteen children died. As a missionary, he made a significant impact for God; yet the Judson "saga" (as it is often called) presents an example of the personal suffering many missionary families endure.

Adoniram was born in Massachusetts, the son of a minister. He was well educated as a young adult, graduating as valedictorian of Brown University in only three years. For a short time he rejected his Christian upbringing. But after attending a new seminary with which his father was involved, Adoniram made a "solemn dedication" of himself to God. After reading an inspiring British mission message, he vowed to be the first American missionary sent from a mission society.

As a young woman, Ann ("Nancy") Hasseltine (1789–1826) had a life-changing spiritual conversion and, as a result, a great burden for the unevangelized. Only three days after Adoniram and Nancy's wedding, the young newlyweds set sail for India. Nancy said she was not going because of "an attachment to an earthly object [i.e., Adoniram]" but because of an "obligation to God," with "full conviction of its being a call." Her life is a testimony of faithfulness as a wife and of total surrender to God's call.

Adoniram and Nancy began their ministry in India, yet they were soon forced to leave that country and go to Burma—which was actually their original first choice. The young couple decided to live among the Burmese people instead of in a secluded mission house. Nancy spoke daily with the women and quickly learned the Burmese language. They built a traditional, Burmese-style *zayat* (an open shelter) where many came to hear the gospel in a relaxed and culturally acceptable atmosphere. And from the start the Judsons actively included the Burmese believers in their work.

The Judsons faced many hardships over the years. While traveling to Asia, Nancy experienced a stillbirth and had to be carried off the ship. In Burma, she gave birth to a son, Roger; and at six months old, he died of a fever. Adoniram was accused of being a spy (during a war between Burma and Britain) and was confined to prison for a year and a half. Nancy pleaded almost daily with the guards for his release. During this time, she gave birth to their third child, Maria. Not long after Adoniram's release from prison, Nancy and then Maria died of a fever.

At this point, Adoniram went into deep mourning for several years. To overcome his grief, he immersed himself in his work. Fourteen years after Nancy's death, he finally completed his Burmese Bible translation.

Eight years after Nancy's death, Judson married a missionary widow named Sarah, and within ten years they had eight children (two died in infancy). Sarah died a year after giving birth to her last child.

During a furlough in America, Judson met a young (half his age) secular-fiction writer named Emily. Judson believed Emily's writing talents could be better utilized for God's purposes and persuaded her to write Sarah's biography. Just a month after meeting, the two became engaged. And only five months later, they were married—which was quite controversial. At the time, different families were raising several of the Judson children, and the separation was causing hardship. In the end, Emily went to Burma with Adoniram, where she assisted him for three years. They also had two children, one of them stillborn.

Adoniram Judson died of an illness on a sea voyage, having served as a missionary for thirty-three years. Despite challenges and opposition, Judson's life made a significant impact for Jesus Christ; and two of the Judson children (by Sarah) became ministers.

Note: Although Adoniram Judson is referred to as "The Father of American Missions," in actuality a former slave named George Liele was America's first foreign missionary. Liele went to Jamaica thirty-three years before the Judsons left for Burma.

ROBERT AND MARY MOFFAT

Patriarch of South African Missions

Family-Friendly Resource:

*   Wholesome Words website: "Robert Moffat: Pioneer Scottish Missionary to South Africa"

(http://www.wholesomewords.org/biography/biorpmoffat.
html); Children's Corner, Missionary Heroes: "Robert Moffat:
Missionary to South Africa" (http://www.wholesomewords.
org/children/heroes/hmoffat.html)

Robert Moffat (1795–1883), known as the "Patriarch of South
Africa Missions," was born in Scotland. His parents imparted to him
a strong missionary zeal as a child. Robert's mother would often read
aloud stories of mission heroes, which led to his decision to become
a missionary. Robert served the Lord for over fifty years in Africa—
with only one furlough—ministering as an evangelist, Bible translator,
educator, explorer, and diplomat.

In 1819, while sharing about his mission work in Cape Town,
Robert met and eventually married Mary Smith (1795–1871), who had
recently come from England. Their marriage was a "happy union"—
not only at the start but also throughout their fifty-three years together.
Mary adapted well to missionary life as she assisted her husband in the
work. Their home was described as "a homey atmosphere with children
always at play." Robert and Mary had ten children, although three died
in childhood. Of the seven who survived, five Moffat children became
actively involved in missionary work in Africa.

Despite their own missionary work, Robert and Mary Moffat are
primarily remembered as the in-laws of David Livingstone, the great
missionary explorer. Originally Robert encouraged Livingstone to go to
the unreached areas of Africa. "On a clear morning," he challenged, "the
smoke of a thousand villages could be seen where the name of Christ
had never been heard." Yet after Livingstone married their daughter
(also named Mary) and pursued that challenge, Robert and Mary often
disagreed with Livingstone's method of fulfilling that call. From the
Moffat's perspective, Livingstone's famous exploratory work often
came at the expense of his family.

After fifty-three years of successful ministry in Africa, Robert
and Mary Moffat returned to England. But within a few months Mary

died. For the thirteen remaining years of his life, Robert ministered as a dynamic missionary spokesman.

"On a clear morning, the smoke of a thousand villages could be seen where the name of Christ had never been heard."

ROBERT MOFFAT (TO DAVID LIVINGSTONE)

The Great Explorers: DAVID AND MARY LIVINGSTONE

The famous explorer . . . and his neglected family

David Livingstone is likely the most famous missionary in history. His exploratory work in Africa was heralded by Christian and secular leaders. He wrote many missionary slogans that continue to be influential today, and his name is nearly synonymous with *missionary*. Yet his famous life was not flawless. It was very difficult for Livingstone to balance his consuming passion for reaching the unreached with the love he had for his family. His wife, Mary, had been raised in Africa and was willing to follow him anywhere; but as their family grew, and especially as they faced pressure from Mary's parents, none of their options seemed to work. It was difficult to travel together, and it was difficult to be separated. In the end, Livingstone chose to concentrate on his missionary calling—a choice that came with a great expense. Livingstone's neglect of his wife and children became a permanent scar on his celebrated missionary biography.

One sad occasion occurred when David Livingstone's nineteen-year-old son, Oswell Livingstone, accompanied a search mission for his father led by Commander Dawson. When their team met up with the returning Henry Stanley (the New York reporter whose search party had found Livingstone), Dawson's search was aborted. Less than a year later, David Livingstone died in Africa . . . and Oswell never saw his father again. Perhaps the young man had not been searching for his famous father, but for his own identity and purpose. Unfortunately, it seems that he found neither.

Excerpts about David Livingstone's Family Life

David Livingstone passionately explained why he had decided to take his pregnant wife and young children with him on a difficult missionary expedition: "It is a venture to take wife and children into a country where fever—African fever—prevails. But who that believes in Jesus would refuse to make a venture for such a Captain?" [8]

Later, Livingstone received a harsh letter from his mother-in-law:

Mary had told me all along that should she be pregnant you would not take her, but let her come out here after you were fairly off . . . but to my dismay I now get a letter—in which she writes, "I must again wend my weary way to the far Interior, perhaps to be confined in the field." O Livingstone, what do you mean—was it not enough that you lost one lovely babe, and scarcely saved the others, while the mother came home threatened with Paralysis? And still you again expose her and them on an exploring expedition? All the world will condemn the cruelty of the thing, to say nothing of the indecorousness of it. A pregnant woman with three little children trailing about with a company of the other sex—through the wilds of Africa among savage men and beasts! Had you found a place to which you wished to go and commence missionary operations the case would be altered. Not one word would I say were it to the mountains of the moon—but to go with an exploring party, the thing is preposterous.

I remain yours in great perturbation,

M. Moffat. [9]

Additional Quotes Regarding Livingstone's Family Priorities:

"Nothing but a strong conviction that the step will tend to the Glory of Christ would make me orphanize my children." Livingstone [10]

Livingstone genuinely loved his children, and in later years regretted he had not spent more time with them. [11]

While Livingstone was on his exciting, exploratory adventures, Mary and the children were "homeless and friendless" and "often living on the edge of poverty in cheap lodgings." It was even rumored among the missionaries that Mary had "lapsed into spiritual darkness and was drowning her misery in alcohol." [12]

In England, Livingstone was given a state funeral at Westminster Abbey, attended by dignitaries from all over the country. It was a day of mourning for his children, who came to say goodbye to the father they had never really known. [13]

GEORGE MÜLLER (1805–1898) AND HIS FAMILY

A family of faith: caring for orphans and reaching the world

Family-Friendly Resources:

- Wholesome Words website: "George Müller: English Evangelist and Philanthropist" (http://www.wholesomewords.org/biography/biorpmueller.html)

- *The Bandit of Ashley Downs: George Müller* (Trailblazer Books), by Dave and Neta Jackson, Bethany House, 1993

- "George Müller: Man of Faith," in *Hero Tales,* Vol. 1, by Dave and Neta Jackson, Bethany House, 2005

- Mission-Minded Monologue Skit (below)

Mission-Minded Monologue Skit #5

Costume: George Müller is wearing a suit and tie, covered by a large overcoat.

Setting: Müller is praying by the grave of his first wife, Mary. For a simple prop, place a cross in the ground and have Müller hold some flowers.

(As he puts the flowers on Mary's grave, Müller begins to pray.) MÜLLER: Oh Father, I thank Thee for Thy many blessings on my life. I thank Thee for all the joys Thou hast given me . . . and Thy wonderful provision . . .

(Müller notices the audience.) Oh, hello there! How are you? My name is George Müller. I am a Christian evangelist and a coordinator of orphanages here in Bristol, England. In fact, I have had the privilege of caring for over 120,000 precious orphan children.

For forty years my beloved wife, Mary, worked alongside me. And were we happy? Verily we were! Did you know that just three weeks after our wedding, Mary and I decided to depend on God alone—and not on the small salary I received as a preacher? Ever since that day, God's provision has never ceased to amaze me.

Our orphanage vision started when we received a letter complaining about the nuisance of all the orphans. And hmmm . . . let me see . . . I was forty years old back then in 1845, and after thirty-six days of prayer God gave us just enough money to get started on our building project!

Oh, and I remember one morning when all the plates and cups and bowls on the table were empty. There was no food in the larder and no money to buy food. The children were standing, waiting for their morning meal, when I said, "Children, you know we must be in time for school." Then lifting up my hand, I prayed, "Dear Father, we thank Thee for what Thou art going to give us to eat."

There was a knock on the door. The baker stood there, and said, "Mr. Müller, I couldn't sleep last night. Somehow I felt you didn't have bread for breakfast, and the Lord wanted me to send you some. So I got up at 2 a.m. and baked some fresh bread, and have brought it."

I thanked the baker, and no sooner had he left, there was a second knock at the door. It was the milkman. He announced that his milk cart had broken down right in front of the orphanage, and he would like to give the children his cans of fresh milk so he could empty his wagon and repair it. [14]

During the last seventeen years, my dear second wife, Susannah, and I have been doing missionary work throughout the world: preaching in the United States, India, Australia, Japan, China, and in forty-two other countries. In fact, we've traveled over 200,000 miles, which is quite extensive for this day and age in which we travel by ship.

People call me "the man who gets things from God." And I can tell you, God has been so very faithful to meet all of our needs.

And He can meet yours too!

George Müller spoke the following words at his wife Mary's funeral. His comments represent a good example of the joy God gives when ministry and family priorities are balanced:

> Were we happy? Verily we were. With every year our happiness increased more and more. I never saw my beloved wife at any time, when I met her unexpectedly anywhere in Bristol, England, without being delighted so to do. I never met her even in the Orphan Houses, without my heart being delighted so to do. Day by day, as we met in our dressing room, at the Orphan Houses, to wash our hands before dinner and tea, I was delighted to meet her, and she was equally pleased to see me. Thousands of times I told her, "My darling, I never saw you at any time, since you became my wife, without my being delighted to see you." [15]

"Unless you intend your wife to be a true missionary, not merely a wife, home-maker, and friend, do not join us."

HUDSON TAYLOR
(TO POTENTIAL MISSIONARY RECRUITS)

Did You Know?

As a testimony to Hudson Taylor's spiritual legacy, several of his children became involved in Christian ministry and missionary work. Even today, his descendants (including Rev. James Hudson Taylor III and his son, Rev. James Hudson Taylor IV) continue in full-time Christian ministry work in Hong Kong and Taiwan.

WILLIAM AND CATHERINE BOOTH

Founders of the Salvation Army—and faithful to their family

Family-Friendly Resources:

- "William and Catherine Booth: Founders of the Salvation Army," in *Hero Tales,* Vol. 1, by Dave and Neta Jackson, Bethany House, 2005

- *Kidnapped by River Rats: William and Catherine Booth* (Trailblazer Books), by Dave and Neta Jackson, Bethany House, 1991

- Mission-Minded Monologue Skit (below)

"General" William (1829–1912) and Catherine (1829–1890) Booth found a powerful mission-minded balance. They had both a fervent passion for unbelievers and a sincere dedication to their family. They founded the Salvation Army and considered their family an asset and a priority in their lives.

"Go straight for souls, and go for the worst."

WILLIAM BOOTH

> "There is an old adage, that
> 'They who rock the cradle rule the world,'
> and they certainly do; but I am afraid that the world has
> been very badly ruled, just because those who rock the
> cradle have not known how to train the child."

CATHERINE BOOTH

Mission-Minded Monologue Skit #6

Costume: Red winter coat, winter hat, scarf, gloves, and a bell next to a hanging red bucket, to look like a Christmastime Salvation Army bell ringer

Setting: A contemporary Salvation Army worker presents this monologue. This person should have a red bucket and a bell. Have him or her begin by ringing the bell and greeting imaginary shoppers.

SALVATION ARMY BELL RINGER (speaking to imaginary shoppers): Merry Christmas, sir! . . . And how are you, ma'am?

(The bell ringer rubs his or her hands together, as if cold, and says quietly, "Hmmm, it's kind of cold today." Then he or she speaks again to imaginary shoppers.) And merry Christmas to you, too! . . . Oh, thank you for your gift! . . . God bless you, sir!

(The bell ringer then turns to speak to the audience.) Oh, hello there! I'm a volunteer for the Salvation Army. You've probably seen folks like me at stores at Christmastime—with our bells and our buckets, raising money to help the poor. But do you know why we're called the "Salvation Army"? Well, let me tell you.

Over a hundred years ago our founder, William Booth, lived in England. General Booth (as we call him) and his wife, Catherine, had a passionate desire to reach the needy and the social outcasts with the Good News of Jesus Christ. In 1865, they began their ministry of street preaching and helping the poor. On ministry banners they wrote the motto "Blood and Fire"—a reference to the blood of Christ and the fire of the Holy Spirit.

Over the years, millions of people, like me, have come to know Jesus through this ministry. And many of us still refer to Mrs. Catherine Booth as the "Mother of the Salvation Army." That amazing woman preached alongside her husband and wrote books and mission pamphlets. On top of all that, the Booths raised eight mighty children who were all workers in the kingdom of God—taking the gospel to many nations, including India, France, Switzerland, and the United States.

One day General Booth had a vision in which he saw a huge ocean filled with drowning people. Some of these people were rescued and put on a rock (which represented people being saved and coming to Jesus). But nearly all the people on the rock were distracted by something, such as making and saving money, amusing themselves with their favorite pastimes, or dressing up in different styles in order to be admired by others. They didn't even care about the other people who were drowning.

William Booth was impacted by the vision, so he wrote down what he saw. I've read it, and it's pretty powerful. It's one of those things that makes a person think. And it really made me realize how much people need Jesus.

Well, I'd better get back to my job here, and I'll let you get back to all you have to do. I do wish you a merry Christmas. And like General William Booth always said, "Go straight for souls, and go for the worst"!

Denny Kenaston reflects upon William and Catherine Booth's exemplary home life:

> William Booth's home was a godly home at its best.
> . . . They had a beautiful balance of two major commands
> in the Word of God. They were to win souls, and to raise

The Mission-Minded Family

your children. God's kingdom is built in these two ways. We are commanded to train up a generation of children who love God with all their heart, mind, and soul. We are also commanded to preach the Gospel and to make disciples in the world around us and in all the world. These two commands can easily get out of balance. History is full of examples of men who won the world and lost their children. On the other hand there are innumerable cases where parents focused on the children, and did nothing to win a lost world around them. This type of parent tends to raise a generation of separatists who quickly become ingrown, legalistic, and unconcerned for their neighbors' lost condition. William and Catherine Booth had a beautiful, balanced vision of both of these commandments. [16]

FANNY CROSBY AND HER FAMILY

A mission-minded vision

Family-Friendly Resources:

- *Fanny Crosby: The Hymn Writer* (Heroes of the Faith Series), by Bernard Ruffin, Barbour Publishing, 1995

- "Rescue the Perishing," a missions hymn by Fanny Crosby (below)

- Mission-Minded Monologue Skit (below)

> "When I get to heaven,
> the first face that shall ever gladden my sight
> will be that of my Savior!"
>
> FANNY CROSBY
> (A MISSION-MINDED HYMN WRITER,
> WHO WAS BLIND)

Mission-Minded Monologue Skit #7

Costume: Fanny is dressed in a long Victorian-style dress with a high-necked collar; her hair is up in a bun; and she is wearing dark, round glasses.

Setting: Fanny is seated in a rocking chair, holding a hymnal or pages of sheet music.

FANNY CROSBY: When I was born, my parents gave me the name Frances Jane Crosby, but they always called me "Fanny."

When I was only six weeks old, I became blind; and when I was just a baby, my father died. But my mother and grandmother, who raised me, believed that God had a special purpose for my life. As a little girl, I was encouraged to be happy, delightful, and confident. I learned to dress myself and fix my own hair; and I loved to ride horses, explore nature, and climb trees. But most of all, I was raised to love Jesus. My grandmother would often read long passages of the Bible to me; and by the time I was ten years old, she had helped me memorize nearly all of the New Testament and at least five books of the Old Testament.

I have always lived in complete darkness. But when I received God's salvation, it was like a "floodtide of celestial light" came into my life. I often volunteer at local ministries; and whenever anyone asks me a question, I enjoy witnessing one to one, as I share the "light" of Jesus.

One time a preacher told me, "I think it is a great pity that the Master did not give you sight when He showered so many other gifts upon you." But I didn't want him to feel sorry for me. Without bitterness, I happily replied, "When I get to heaven, the first face that shall ever gladden my sight will be that of my Savior!"

Although I cannot see, God has shown me His vision and purpose for my life. I have always loved music and poetry; and over the years He helped me compose over eight thousand hymns and hundreds of poems, including many that convey the need for missions. To share a little more of my heart, I would like to read one of these hymns, which is about sharing the gospel with the lost. This hymn is called "Rescue the Perishing." As you listen, remember that God has a special purpose for your life too!

RESCUE THE PERISHING

A missions hymn, by Fanny Crosby (1820–1915)

Rescue the perishing,
Care for the dying,
Snatch them in pity from sin and the grave;
Weep o'er the erring one,
Lift up the fallen,
Tell them of Jesus, the mighty to save.

Rescue the perishing,
Care for the dying;
Jesus is merciful,
Jesus will save.

Rescue the perishing,
Duty demands it;
Strength for thy labor the Lord will provide;
Back to the narrow way
Patiently win them;
Tell the poor wand'rer a Savior has died.

> Rescue the perishing,
> Care for the dying;
> Jesus is merciful,
> Jesus will save.[17]

C. T. AND PRISCILLA STUDD

Recruited hundreds of new missionaries

Family-Friendly Resources:

- Wholesome Words, Children's Corner: "C. T. Studd: Cricketer and Pioneer" (http://www.wholesomewords.org/children/biostuddcc.html)

- *C. T. Studd: No Retreat* (Christian Heroes: Then & Now Series), by Janet and Geoff Benge, YWAM Publishing, 2005

> "The light that shines the farthest shines the brightest nearest home."
>
> C. T. STUDD (AN IRONIC QUOTE)

Charles Thomas (C. T.) Studd (1860–1931) was fervent about world missions and reaching the lost for Jesus Christ. He wrote, "We do need to be intense, and our intensity must ever increase." Yet his ever-increasing and unbalanced intensity eventually led to his downfall.

C. T. was led to the Lord by his father, who dramatically exchanged a life of horse racing for preaching the gospel. C. T. committed his life to Christ and to missionary service. During the Student Volunteer Movement, he and six friends—known as the Cambridge Seven—left England to become missionaries to China.

In China, he met Priscilla Stewart, a missionary with the Salvation Army. The two were soon married, and within ten years they had four daughters. During the early years their individual ministries in China began to grow, as C. T. helped opium addicts and Priscilla reached out to women. Once, upon receiving a large inheritance, he gave it away. Studd explained, "If Jesus Christ be God and died for me, no sacrifice can be too great for me to make for Him."

In 1900, after six years of successfully preaching about missions throughout Europe and the United States, Studd moved his family to India, where their focus shifted (very unhappily) from evangelism to ministry to English-speaking believers.

At age fifty-three, Studd felt God calling him to the "heart of Africa." Priscilla strongly objected and was overwhelmed by the decision. Physically, she was unable to go; yet he strongly felt that the work of the ministry had to come before the needs of the family. From 1910 until the time of Priscilla's death, in 1929, the two were together for less than two years. Only once during his eighteen years in Africa did C. T. return home to England (where she had remained). Even when he learned that his wife had suffered serious heart complications, he refused to turn back.

Studd's ministry was known for being radical, but his views became excessive. He believed in total commitment, which meant "no diversions, no days off, no recreation." He believed laziness was a sin (which could lead to damnation) and often worked relentless eighteen-hour days. He lived with Spartan simplicity and expected everyone around him to make extreme sacrifices. In the end, Studd began to take morphine to counterbalance the strain caused from overworking; and his own mission organization had to dismiss him. It was a great shame, and within a few weeks he died.

Though his personal life and family were sacrificed, C. T. Studd left a lasting impact on missions. He recruited hundreds of committed volunteers, and his son-in-law (who honored him, yet acknowledged his errors) continued WEC International: Worldwide Evangelization Crusade. This ministry has remained strong in pioneer missions, Bible translation, church planting, and evangelizing unreached people. They also produce *Operation World*, a much-used, country-by-country, world-mission prayer guide.

"Some wish to live within the
sound of church or chapel bell. I want to run
a rescue shop within a yard of hell!"

C. T. STUDD

C. T. STUDD SPEAKS TO HIS DAUGHTER FROM HIS DEATHBED

As he was dying, C. T. Studd conveyed to his daughter his sincere heart for Jesus. While bidding farewell, the old man said, "Pauline, I would like to give you something before you go." He looked about him as if to find a suitable parting gift. His table held some gadgets; and he had a few boxes on poles (to keep them from the termites), containing some clothes and a few small possessions. From the roof hung a banjo for leading the singing and some pots for cooking. Then he quietly said, "But really, I have nothing to give you because I gave it all to Jesus long ago."

T. L. AND DAISY OSBORN

Mission-minded mass evangelist

Family-Friendly Resource:

*   *Soulwinning: A Classic on Biblical Christianity*, by T. L. Osborn (Harrison House, 1994)

They never received a "call" to ministry, but for over fifty years T. L. and Daisy Osborn have ministered through open-air mass evangelism to millions of people. (Daisy passed away in 1995.) Their ministry films and videos have been translated into nearly eighty languages, and their literature has been published in 132 languages and dialects—influencing multitudes to believe the gospel of Jesus Christ. T. L. and Daisy Osborn have written many books and inspiring articles concerning evangelism and world missions, including *Soulwinning.*

📖 GOD'S HIDDEN INHERITANCE

An excerpt from T. L. Osborn's 1964 book, *Frontier Evangelism*

The treasure of one thousand million heathen souls lies hidden in the remote fields of the earth today and within the reach of the present generation of the church. This priceless treasure is lying as an unclaimed inheritance. It is waiting to be possessed by men [and women] of vision, of faith and of courage who will "sell all" and dedicate themselves to buy this field. . . . The responsibility to invade these enormous frontiers and possess this treasure demands unselfish and sacrificial devotion to the cause for which Jesus died—the evangelization of the world. Paul's life was constantly in peril as he advanced to possess the heathen treasure of his generation. Today, rugged men [and women] of courageous faith must arise to the challenge of this generation. They must possess this inheritance regardless of peril, regardless of sacrifice, regardless of resistance.

Where are the rugged pioneers of faith today who will respond to this challenge?

Where are the men of vision who are no longer content to rest in the security of an established congregation and salary?

Where are those who look with keen anticipation to the unprecedented possibilities of pioneering heathen frontiers for Christ?

Where are the fearless preacher's wives who will stand by the side of their husbands while they blaze new trails to reach the lost?

Where are the brave men who are tired of the monotony of religious competition?

Where are those who yearn to proclaim Christ in a field that has not been burnt over by the hordes of religious opportunities and gospel commercializers?

Where are the courageous mothers who will forsake the established conveniences of a modern civilization to take their children in an advance to stake unclaimed treasures among the souls of the heathen?[18]

"One Way—Jesus; One Job—Evangelism"

T. L. AND DAISY OSBORN'S MOTTO

REINHARD AND ANNI BONNKE

German founder of Christ for All Nations

Family-Friendly Resource:

* *Evangelism by Fire: Igniting Your Passion for the Lost*, by Reinhard Bonnke (Full Flame, 2002)

Reinhard Bonnke grew up in Germany as a pastor's son. He gave his life to the Lord when he was nine years old; and before becoming a teenager Reinhard felt called to the mission fields of Africa. In 1969, he and his young wife, Anni, and their baby son went to Maseru, Lesotho. For seven long years Reinhard and Anni ministered as traditional missionaries, but seeing "little fruit" for their efforts frustrated them.

Reinhard kept having visions of a "blood-washed Africa" and mass-evangelism outreaches. But as he shared what he believed to be God's calling, others criticized him and claimed he was full of pride. Bonnke submitted his ideas to God in prayer; and he believed the Lord responded by saying, "If you don't do it, I'll just have to find someone else." From that time on, Reinhard began holding mass-evangelism meetings, initially in a tent accommodating eight hundred people.

Today Reinhard Bonnke leads open-air outreaches, throughout the world and especially in Africa, that draw crowds of more than half a million people in a single meeting! Many churches join together to support these citywide events, since salvation through the sacrifice of Christ is emphasized. Bonnke's Christ for All Nations has offices in Africa, Germany, the United Kingdom, Canada, Singapore, and the

United States. He has written several missions books, including one of my favorites: *Evangelism by Fire.*

> "Cool, casual Christianity will accomplish nothing. Our . . . most urgent need is the flaming message of the cross—now and not at our leisure."
>
> REINHARD BONNKE

DON AND CAROL RICHARDSON

Missionaries to New Guinea

Family-Friendly Resources:

- *Peace Child* (YWAM Publishing, 2003) and *Eternity in Their Hearts* (Regal Books; revised edition, 1984), by Don Richardson

- *Peace Child*, the film (Gospel Communications, 1974). This powerful movie, available on DVD, shares the amazing testimony of Don and Carol Richardson. There is brief nudity, in the native fashion. A missions classic.

In 1955, a young couple responded to a specific missionary call to reach the Sawi people, a cannibalistic tribe of headhunters in New Guinea. Don and Carol Richardson and their baby arrived in the remote village in a simple dugout canoe. They didn't know what to expect, but they knew they were obeying God's direction for their lives.

After learning the people's language, Don and Carol shared about God's love. Yet their noble attempts seemed completely futile. The savage tribe honored treachery, so when the people heard the story of Christ, they believed Judas—not Jesus—was the true hero. It was not until the Richardsons discovered an important aspect of Sawi culture, called "the peace child," that they were able to share the gospel effectively. The Sawi people believed that if an enemy tribe offered to give them one of their own babies, as a sign of peace, then that enemy tribe could genuinely be trusted. Don used this analogy to share about the birth of Jesus, and finally the Sawi people understood God's Good News.

The Richardsons lived for fifteen years among this primitive tribe in Irian Jaya, and more than half of the Sawi people accepted Jesus Christ as their Savior and Lord. As a nurse, Carol ministered to the physical needs of the people—at times treating nearly 2,500 patients each month. Together, Don and Carol worked on a Bible translation project and completed a Sawi translation of the New Testament. Using traditional building techniques, their ministry built a huge "Sawidome" church (seating over one thousand people) to be used for Christian work.

In Don Richardson's book *Peace Child,* he shares this moving story; and in *Eternity in Their Hearts,* he encourages missionaries to look for "redemptive cultural analogies." Richardson has also studied and written about the needs of the Muslim world, and he is a prominent spokesman for world missions.

More Examples of Mission-Minded Legacies

Around the world today, there are many powerful examples of mission-minded families with generational legacies that are impacting the world.

- As featured in the movie *End of the Spear*, **Steve Saint** (the son of Nate Saint, a famous missionary martyred while attempting to reach an isolated tribe in Ecuador) is seeing tremendous ministry results among this remote people.

As the founder of I-TEC, Indigenous People's Technology and Education Center, Steve and his family continue in his missionary heritage through his ministry, writing, and speaking.

- **Walter and Valerie Shepard**, along with their children, live and minister in the Democratic Republic of the Congo. For Walt, this is a return to the country of his youth, where his parents served as missionaries. For Valerie, the daughter of well-known missionaries Jim and Elisabeth Elliot, this is a continuation of a lifelong missions call, fulfilled both as a stay-at-home mother and as a missionary.

- **Dave and Neta Jackson** are mission-minded authors, motivating multitudes of children and young people through their family-friendly missionary books, such as the *Hero Tales* books and the Trailblazer series.

- **Rick and Kay Warren**, using the principles of Rick's book *The Purpose-Driven Life*, impact many people throughout the world for Jesus. They donate 90 percent of their book proceeds to local and international mission projects, especially focusing on the AIDS epidemic in Rwanda.

- **Ken Ham** was inspired by his father's deep love for the Bible and his own convictions about creation. His family sent him as a missionary from Australia to America, where he founded Answers in Genesis, emphasizing the authority of God's Word.

- After graduating from Oral Roberts University, where the mission is to "raise up students to hear My voice, to go where My light is dim, where My voice is heard small . . . even to the uttermost bounds of the earth," **Ron and Katie Luce** founded Teen Mania, a world outreach impacting many young people.

- **Loren and Darlene Cunningham** were both raised in strong mission-minded families. They founded Youth With A Mission (YWAM), one of the world's largest missionary organizations.

- **Leo and Phyllis Kaylor** responded to General MacArthur's plea for missionaries following World War II. For fifty-five years they have served as missionaries in Japan—planting churches, training Christian workers, and raising and homeschooling their six children (all of whom learned to speak Japanese fluently and have a fervent mission-minded heart). Today, Leo and Phyllis Kaylor's children, grandchildren, and great-grandchildren are grateful for their strong Christian heritage, and several are involved in the Kaylors' mission work in Japan.

Part III

Our Mission-Minded Vision

CHAPTER 5

Enjoying Missions throughout the Year

International Holiday Ideas

Throughout the year, acknowledging international holidays can give our families an insight into our world's need for Jesus. These vibrant festivities are filled with colorful expression, yet often these traditions are rooted in false religion and fear.

As your family looks at current traditions around the world each month, you can utilize these specific days to target different people groups for prayer and to increase your family's mission-minded vision. You may even want to commemorate some of these days. However, I am *not* encouraging your family to celebrate evil or pagan holidays. This international holiday list is simply to help your family learn about world cultures and to regularly remind you about the need for specific mission-minded prayer.

🌐 TEACHING OPPORTUNITY

Make a Mission-Minded Family Calendar

Get out your family calendar, and take a moment to write down the names of these holidays on their respective dates. Throughout the year, you can then come back to this section of *The Mission-Minded Family* to read about each holiday and pray accordingly.

JANUARY

1 • New Year's Day, International—Around much of the world, this day is celebrated as a time of new beginnings. Many people make New Year's "resolutions," or promises, for the coming year.

As mission-minded believers, pray for and seek God's direction for the new year and take time to evaluate and realign your priorities.

6 • Epiphany, International—In many countries throughout the world, this day is celebrated to remember the wise men who came to bring gifts of gold, frankincense, and myrrh to the Christ child, Jesus. In Spain, children receive gifts on this day instead of on Christmas. Children put hay in their shoes and find the hay replaced with treats the next morning.

Pray for the people of Spain to recognize Jesus Christ as Savior and Messiah, just as the wise men did.

14 • Pongal, India—In southern India, this day marks the beginning of a four-day harvest festival. The people gather to watch a pot of newly harvested rice boil. If it boils quickly, the people believe it is a sign of a prosperous new year.

Pray for a mighty *spiritual* harvest in India.

Martin Luther King Day, United States (date varies)—Dr. Martin Luther King Jr., born and raised in Atlanta, Georgia, was a Christian minister and a civil rights leader. King was active in seeing segregation laws in the South abolished, and in 1964 he received the Nobel Peace Prize. He was assassinated in 1968. The third Monday of January is set aside as a national holiday to remember King's leadership and the importance of civil rights.

Pray for harmony and love between different races and nationalities and for God to give you love and compassion for other people groups.

JANUARY/FEBRUARY

Chinese New Year (date varies)—In China, families clean their homes to prepare for the new year and to rid their lives of any misfortunes or bad luck from the previous year. People wear new shoes and clothing and often decorate with red candles, symbolizing good luck. Processions are held, often led by a huge dragon, also symbolizing good luck. Firecrackers are set off (sometimes to rid the area of evil spirits), and families participate in gift giving and meals.

Pray for an outpouring of God's Holy Spirit and revival in China. Pray that the Chinese people would not trust in superstitions and luck, but in the newness of life found only in Jesus Christ.

Eid-al-Fitr, Islamic countries (date varies)—In the Islamic month of Ramadan, devout Muslims fast from both food and water during the daylight hours (fasting during Ramadan is one of the five pillars of Islam). At sunset on the last day of the month, the people celebrate the breaking of the fast (Eid-al-Fitr) with celebrations, food, and gifts.

Pray for Muslim people around the world to recognize Jesus as God's Son and accept Him as their personal Savior.

FEBRUARY

14 • Valentine's Day—This holiday, also known as St. Valentine's Day, was named after two early Christian martyrs named Valentine and is observed by Western and Western-influenced cultures. In the United States and some other countries, cards and gifts are given to friends, sweethearts, and family members to express love.

Pray for contemporary Christians who are being persecuted for their faith in Jesus Christ. See www.persecution.com for updated reports from Voice of the Martyrs, or read a selection from the powerful book *Jesus Freaks*, by dc Talk.

STARTLING MISSION-MINDED FACT

From Neal Pirolo's 1991 book, *Serving as Senders*

> On just one day, February 14, Americans spend over 700 million dollars to say "I love you" with Valentine's Day cards. Less than that is spent in the whole month of February (and in each of the other months) to tell a lost and dying world that God loves them!

FEBRUARY/MARCH

Holi, India (date varies)—Children from India celebrate the coming of spring by showering each other with brightly colored water and paint powders. Huge bonfires are lit to "burn away" the old season.

Pray for people bound in Hinduism all throughout India to find new life and forgiveness from their sins through Jesus Christ.

MARCH

17 • St. Patrick's Day, Ireland—Patrick was the first Christian missionary to Ireland (see the mini-biography below). In the United States, celebrations include city parades, Irish cultural celebrations, and the wearing of green.

Pray for peace in Ireland, especially between Protestants and Catholics. Pray for the true message of salvation to spread throughout Ireland and for missionaries who are sharing the gospel in Ireland today.

WHO WAS ST. PATRICK?

Born in Britain, "Saint" Patrick (c. AD 389–461) is widely known as the first Christian missionary to the Irish people. Patrick actually went to Ireland twice—first as a slave and later as a missionary. When he was sixteen, he was captured and taken to Ireland, where he remained until he escaped and returned to his homeland. While in Ireland, young Patrick repented of his sinful, backslidden condition. Sometime later, back in Britain, he received a vision from God calling him to return to the Irish people to proclaim the gospel of Christ. Patrick obeyed God's call and went back.

For the remainder of his life, Patrick ministered among the heathen tribes of Ireland—confronting idolatry and sorcery, converting many to Jesus Christ, and baptizing thousands of people. Tradition says he used the three-leaf clover to teach the unity of the Father, Son, and Holy Spirit.

Patrick is known today as the patron saint of Ireland, and throughout the world people celebrate "St. Patrick's Day" during the month of March.

MARCH/APRIL

Passover, Israel (date varies)—This Jewish celebration remembers how God delivered the ancient Hebrews from slavery in Egypt as the death angel "passed over" their homes. A special dinner, called the Seder, includes unleavened bread (matzo), lamb, and bitter herbs. Jesus celebrated the Passover every year; and through His death on the cross, He fulfilled it. God has provided freedom from the bitterness of sin and eternal death, for "Christ, our Passover Lamb, has been sacrificed for us" (1 Corinthians 5:7 NLT).

Pray for Jews around the world to recognize Jesus Christ (Yeshua) as their promised Messiah.

Holy Week, International (date varies)—Christians around the world celebrate the death and resurrection of Jesus Christ during Holy Week. In many Latin American countries there are huge processions in which large statues of Jesus and other religious relics are carried through the streets. There is little or no mention of the resurrection in many of these settings. In other places, such as in the Philippines, men actually allow themselves to be nailed to a cross— done as "penance" (a religious self-effort to pay part of the punishment for their sins).

Pray for people around the world, especially for those in Latin America, to hear of the resurrection and to receive God's salvation through faith in Jesus Christ—not by their own works.

The Mission-Minded Family

APRIL/MAY

Hana Matsuri, Buddha's Birthday (date varies)—Throughout Asia, Buddhists celebrate the birthday of the founder of their religion. In Japan, people celebrate Hana Matsuri on April 8 by bringing flowers to shrines and holding parades. In Southeast Asia, the date for this holiday (known as Vesak) varies. People decorate buildings with lights and paper lanterns and hold rocket festivals.

Pray for the salvation of Buddhists around the world. Intercede for their spiritual eyes to be opened and for the light of the gospel to reach them so that they can turn to the living Savior, Jesus Christ.

MAY

1 • May Day, International—Many different holidays are celebrated around the world on the first day of May, including ancient pagan celebrations and the more recent International Workers' Day. A tradition in America is to secretly deliver flowers to friends and neighbors. You may want to help your children bless your neighbors with flowers and homemade cards that share the love of Jesus Christ. Some who practice Roman Catholicism give special veneration and honor to the Virgin Mary on this day.

Pray for the salvation of your neighbors and for those who hope and trust in Mary for their salvation—that their faith would be in Jesus alone.

1 • Lei Day, Hawaii—Throughout Hawaii, people make and wear leis (flower necklaces) with tropical flowers and perform traditional dances. The first Lei Day was held on May 1, 1928; and later the phrase "May Day is Lei Day" was coined.

Pray for Christians throughout Hawaii to share the love of Jesus on this day and to glorify the Lord through traditional Hawaiian dances.

5 • Children's Day, Japan—Kites in the shape of fish are flown to signify strength and courage. Children throughout the country participate in religious ceremonies where they are blessed by their parents. (Many other nations celebrate International Children's Day on June 1.)

Pray for the children of Japan to turn from false religions and ancestral worship to find faith in Jesus Christ. Pray for these children to know how much Jesus loves them.

Mother's Day, International (date varies)—A day for honoring mothers is celebrated on various dates throughout the world. Mother's Day is celebrated on the second Sunday of May in many countries. People often take their moms out to lunch and give them cards, flowers, and gifts.

Thank God for your mother, especially if she is a godly influence in your life.

Pray today for orphan children throughout the world who do not have a mother, that God would care for them and lead them to a family that can help them or adopt them. Pray also for any mothers and grandmothers you know who are not believers (for example, in your extended family or neighborhood).

25 • African Liberation Day, Africa—African countries that are members of the Organization of African Unity celebrate their independence on this day through traditional dances, celebrations, sports, and rallies.

Pray for peace throughout the continent of Africa and for revival to spread to those who have yet to hear of God's gift of freedom in Christ.

JUNE

Father's Day, International (date varies)—A day for commemorating fatherhood and honoring fathers is celebrated on various dates throughout the world. Father's Day is celebrated on the third Sunday of June in many countries. People give their dads gifts and do fun things with them.

Thank the Lord for your father, especially if he is a godly example in your life.

Pray today for the lost, especially in your nation, that they would come to know their heavenly Father.

JULY

1 • Canada Day, Canada—On this day, Canadians celebrate the birthday of their country with parades, fireworks, and barbecues.

Pray for the people of Canada to recognize their need for God and for Christians throughout this country to reach the lost.

4 • Independence Day, United States—Americans commemorate the signing of the Declaration of Independence on July 4, 1776, by celebrating with parades, fireworks, and picnics.

Pray for the citizens and leaders of the United States to live out their Christian roots and to be mission-minded people.

14 • Bastille Day, France—On July 14, 1789, the French Revolution began with the storming of the Bastille (a royal prison). This was the beginning of freedom from oppression by the monarchy. The French people celebrate with parades, fireworks, and dancing in the streets.

Pray that those in France who aren't believers would recognize the devil's oppression and desire God's true freedom, found only in Jesus Christ.

JUNE/JULY/AUGUST

Sun Dance, Native Americans—Across the US and Canadian plains, Native Americans (or First Nation people) perform an ancient Sun Dance ceremony honoring the buffalo.

Pray for Native American people to recognize the living God who created everything. Pray that they don't view Christianity as only a "white man's religion," but as God's salvation for them.

SEPTEMBER

11 • Enkutatash, Ethiopia—After the rainy season has ended each year, the people of Ethiopia celebrate their new year on September 11, which is the first day of the Ethiopian month of Meskerem. Children gather flowers and go from house to house, singing songs and giving flowers. In return, the children receive coins or candy.

Read in Acts 8 how Philip shared the gospel with an Ethiopian official. Pray for peace, evangelism, and spiritual revival throughout modern-day Ethiopia.

16 • Independence Day, Mexico—On September 16, 1810, Father Miguel Hidalgo first sounded a call for Mexican independence from Spain. The revolution ended in 1821, with Mexico becoming a free country. On the evening of September 15, Mexicans gather in public squares to hear a call for independence at eleven o'clock, which is followed by fireworks and dancing.

Pray for the people of Mexico to hear God calling them to Himself. Pray for missionaries and national ministers throughout Mexico to preach God's freedom through Jesus Christ.

SEPTEMBER/OCTOBER

Rosh Hashanah, Israel (date varies)—At the beginning of the Jewish New Year a ram's horn, or shofar, is blown in the synagogues. This is a festive time of special food and family celebrations as the Jewish people reflect on the new year.

Pray for Jews throughout the world to recognize Jesus (Yeshua) as their Messiah.

Tet Trung Thu, Vietnam (date varies)—This celebration of the moon comes at the time of the harvest moon. Mooncakes are eaten, and children make lanterns in the shapes of animals and other objects. At night, the children carry their lanterns in processions.

Pray for God's light to shine throughout Vietnam and for many to come to know Jesus Christ, through whom God created the sun, moon, and stars.

OCTOBER

9 • Hangul Nal, Korea—On October 9, South Koreans celebrate the creation of the Korean alphabet in the fifteenth century. North Koreans celebrate Hangul Day on January 15.

Children take part in calligraphy contests instead of their regular school classes.

This is a good day to have a handwriting contest with a special missions verse. Pray for the Lord to pour out His Holy Spirit on children in both South Korea (where the Christian church is strong and mission oriented) and North Korea (where there is great spiritual need).

31 • Halloween, Western countries—Halloween was originally a pagan festival observed by the Celts of Ireland and Britain. It was later transformed to the "Hallowed Eve" of All Saints' Day (November 1), a holiday in which Roman Catholics and some Protestants remember believers who have died. In the United States, children carve pumpkins on Halloween, dress in costumes (sometimes as witches, ghosts, devils, or other evil characters), and go "trick-or-treating" throughout neighborhoods to receive candy.

Satanic rituals reportedly take place on Halloween, and people attempt to make contact with the dead. Pray for wisdom as a Christian family, school, or church to discern good from evil. Realize Satan is real and not something to have "fun" with or to make light of. Many churches utilize this day to have a "harvest party" or dramatic outreach. Pray for eyes to be opened to the reality of evil and for many to come to Christ.

OCTOBER/NOVEMBER

Diwali, India (date varies)—Throughout India, people celebrate this "Festival of Lights" by placing lamps in their homes and windows and on roofs and roads. They believe that these beautiful lamps welcome Lakshmi, the goddess of good luck. People clean their homes and make designs with colored powder on their floors.

Pray for the people of India to turn from this false religion and to recognize Jesus as the true Light of the World.

NOVEMBER

Loy Krathong, Thailand (date varies)—For hundreds of years, the people of Thailand have celebrated this festival of floating leaf cups. On the night of the full moon in November, people make little boats out of banana leaves and flowers and place a candle inside. They take their decorative rafts to a river, light the candle, make a wish, and then put the leaf boat in the water. If the candle stays lit until the boat disappears from sight, they believe that the wish will come true.

Pray for the people of Thailand to put their hope and faith in Jesus, the light of the world.

Thanksgiving, United States (date varies)—The Pilgrim settlers of Plymouth Colony in Massachusetts established a holiday of feasting and praising God after their first harvest in 1621. They were especially thankful for Squanto, the Native American who taught them how to catch fish and grow corn. Many US presidents proclaimed a national day of thanksgiving to God. In 1939, President Franklin Roosevelt set the date for the holiday on the fourth Thursday of November. Canada observes a similar national Thanksgiving holiday on the second Monday in October.

Be thankful for God's blessings in your life. Pray for revival in North America, especially among Native Americans (or First Nations people).

NOVEMBER/DECEMBER

Hanukkah (or Chanukah) (date varies)—About two hundred years before the birth of Jesus, Syrian Greek rulers disgraced the Jewish temple and then ordered the Jews to worship Greek gods. For three years the people of Israel fought for freedom and finally defeated their enemies. The Jews cleansed their temple and then lit a special candelabra called a menorah. They had enough oil to last only one day, but the menorah stayed lit, supernaturally, for eight days. Throughout the world, Jews celebrate the "Festival of Lights" by lighting candles each night for eight nights. Celebrations also include giving gifts, eating traditional foods, and playing games.

Whenever you see a menorah, pray for peace in Israel and for Jewish families to come to know Jesus as their Savior and Messiah.

DECEMBER

13 • St. Lucia Day, Sweden—In Sweden (and other Scandinavian countries), there is a legend of St. Lucia, a Sicilian girl who gave away her dowry to feed the poor. She is known as the Queen of Light. Coming at the time when the nights are long in Scandinavia, this holiday also celebrates the ability of light to overcome darkness. Every year, the oldest girl in each family plays the part of St. Lucia. In the morning, she puts on a white dress with a ring of candles on her head and brings coffee and special rolls to her parents.

Pray for the people of Sweden to come to know Christ as the Light of the World. Pray for missionaries and ministers in this country to bring the light of Jesus to those who are spiritually poor.

16–24 • Las Posadas, Latin America—Throughout Mexico and Latin America, families celebrate Christmas by acting out the story of Mary and Joseph searching for lodging. This scene is reenacted each evening from December 16 to 24. In some areas children carry nativity figures of Mary and Joseph, while in other areas a man and woman wear costumes to look like them. As they go from house to house, asking for a place to stay, a procession forms behind them. Finally, "Mary and Joseph" arrive at a house, are allowed in, and are placed by a manger. Everyone then joins in a celebration, complete with a piñata for the children.

Pray that the gospel spreads throughout Latin America as people open the door of their hearts to accept Jesus Christ as their Lord and Savior.

25 • Christmas, International—The celebration of Jesus' birth is an important time for us as Christian believers. It is a time to remember Christ's love and sacrifice in coming to this earth, a time to thank God for His salvation, and a great time to share God's love with others.

Throughout the Christmas season, use evergreen trees to remind your children of God's gift of everlasting life through the cross of Calvary. As you see Christmas lights and candles, remember that Jesus is the Light of the World and that we are to be lights for Him. As you receive presents, remember the gifts of the wise men—and the greatest gift of God's salvation. Discuss how the birth of Jesus declared His coming for all people: rich and poor, Jew and Gentile, those near and those far away.

Thank the Lord Jesus for coming to earth to be our Savior!

MISSION-MINDED CHRISTMAS CAROLS

- "Joy to the World"
- "Hark! The Herald Angels Sing"
- "Go Tell It on the Mountain"
- "Silent Night"

"For God so loved the world, that he gave his only begotten Son, that whosoever believeth in him should not perish, but have everlasting life."

JOHN 3:16 (KJV)

LOTTIE MOON: SHE GAVE EVERYTHING ... ON CHRISTMAS

Missionary to China (1840–1912)

Does your family know about Lottie Moon? In Southern Baptist churches, her testimony of missionary service and sacrifice is something of a legend. She is the namesake of a yearly international Christmas missions offering; and her beautiful yet sad story of sacrificial giving has been retold each year, inspiring many (especially during the Christmas season) to a deeper commitment to missions.

Charlotte "Lottie" Moon grew up in Virginia as a wealthy, cultivated Southern girl, well educated by private tutors. She was the third of seven children. When she was thirteen, her father was killed in a riverboat accident. Although petite in body, she was strong in mind and spirit. Lottie became a missionary to China, and for thirty-nine years she ministered faithfully. She wore traditional Chinese clothing, adopted the language and customs of the people, and did all she could to share the gospel of Jesus Christ. She also wrote influential letters back home about the world's great need to support missions and established a new Christmas missions offering.

In 1912, during a time of war and famine in China, Lottie gave and gave, not counting the personal cost. She urgently wrote home for help, but to no avail; the mission board was heavily in debt and unable to send anything. Lottie's sharing of her personal finances and food with anyone in need severely damaged her physical and mental health. Fellow missionaries became alarmed and arranged for her to be sent home. However, as her ship docked in Japan, Lottie died . . . on Christmas Eve.

"I Gave Myself"

It was Christmas, and the Liberian Christians had been asked this year, instead of receiving gifts, to help carry the gospel to others. As in many mission fields, they brought, not money, but produce. Presently, the great plates were piled high with offerings of rice, cocoa, bananas, palm nuts, pineapple, and cassava.

There was a moment's pause . . .

Slowly a twelve-year-old boy walked forward and solemnly placed his feet in one of the plates.

Afterward, when the missionary questioned him, the boy said, "We are very poor. I did not have anything else to give . . . so I gave myself."

I'll Be Home for Christmas?

It was only a few days before Christmas as Bernie May, a pilot for Wycliffe Bible Translators, successfully delivered emergency medical supplies to the isolated Amazon village. Now he eagerly anticipated being back with his wife and children in their South American home-away-from-home. Yet as the evening grew dark, he knew he would not be able to fly out until the morning.

With his pontoon plane waiting on the river, Bernie arranged for temporary protection for the night. But then . . . it began to rain.

The rain continued, even up until Christmas Eve, as the missionary felt increasingly depressed by his misfortune. His wife, Nancy, and their boys were six hours away; and by this time, they would have received his radio message: he would not be home for Christmas.

As a family, they had prepared their hearts to be separated from their loved ones and friends, but it was Christmas Eve . . . and they were now separated from even each other.

Back in Pennsylvania, everyone would be coming home from church—to the sound of caroling, the smell of roasting turkey, and the sight of falling snow.

But where was God's missionary? Here he was . . . stuck in a remote jungle . . . in a makeshift shelter . . . in the pouring rain . . . alone.

In Ruth Tucker's book *From Jerusalem to Irian Jaya*, Bernie May tells of his experience:

> "Oh God," I moaned, "I'm in the wrong place." . . . But that night, under my mosquito net, I had a visitation from God—something like those shepherds must have had on the hills of Bethlehem. There were no angels, and no bright lights. But as I lay there in my hammock, desperately homesick, I felt I heard God say, "My son, this is what Christmas is all about. Jesus left heaven and on Christmas morning He woke up in the 'wrong place'—a stable in Bethlehem. Christmas means leaving home, not going home. My only begotten Son did not come home for Christmas—He left home to be with you."

CHAPTER 6

Becoming Prayer Champions

We all know, at least in our heads, that prayer is important. Yet how many of us honestly believe that *our* prayers, the simple prayers of *our* far-from-perfect family, can really make a difference? If we could comprehend, deep down in our spirits, the true power of prayer, we would *all* pray more—and the difference would radically impact our lives and the lives of everyone around us.

This chapter focuses on becoming a spiritually effective family through *intercessory prayer*, helping God's purposes to be released and fulfilled on the earth. To learn about encouraging children in *personal prayer* and helping them establish their own special quiet time with God, please see the chapter on prayer in *The Mission-Minded Child*.

Q. What is the difference between "personal prayer" and "intercessory prayer"?

Personal prayer is a vital part of our daily Christian walk. The primary purpose of our personal prayer life is to know our wonderful Lord and to grow closer to Him. This discipline (and this daily time of delight) flows from a constantly growing and ever-changing relationship with the never-changing God. Our time of personal prayer and communion with God is a vital expression of our love and worship.

Intercessory prayer is praying on behalf of someone else. The primary purposes are to spiritually support and defend God's purposes here on earth and to help "stand in the gap" for His will to be accomplished. In Ezekiel 22:30, the Lord says, "I sought for a man among them who would make a wall, and stand in the gap before Me on behalf of the land, that I should not destroy it; but I found no one."

God is all-powerful; yet He has established a self-imposed requirement that human beings pray in order for His will on earth to be accomplished. Our prayers can make a difference, and there is tremendous strength in the power of agreement in prayer as a family. Our children are people too. (Isn't that a revelation?) Just think what that could mean! I believe that even a child's prayer—especially when that child has been trained in the truth of God's Word—can fulfill God's requirement just as strategically as an adult's prayer. And perhaps, because of a child's simple faith and absolute trust, God might even see his or her prayers as *more* effective than ours.

There is great strength when a husband and wife agree together in prayer; and when an entire family unites in corporate prayer and intercession, it's *really* powerful! As a praying, mission-minded family, we can "work with God" to help see His purposes come to pass—in individuals, in situations, and even in the nations of the world.

What an enormous privilege and responsibility.

"Give me the love that leads the way,
The faith that nothing can dismay,
The hope no disappointments fire,
The passion that will burn like fire!"

AMY CARMICHAEL

Intercession Keys

Three keys of intercession that can help our families to become prayer champions for God are found in James 5:16: "The effective, fervent prayer of a righteous man avails much."

- Key 1—God is looking for "righteous" people to pray.

- Key 2—Our prayers must be effective.

- Key 3—Our prayers must be fervent.

Q. What does it mean to stand "righteous" before God?

As a family, we're very aware of our differences and our faults. We've all sinned, and we need to acknowledge that no one on earth can stand blameless before our perfect, holy, and awesome God. No matter how good we try to be, our own works are nothing but filthy rags in His sight (see Isaiah 64:6). To pray effectively as a family, we need to grasp the importance of the "fear of the Lord." We don't need to be "afraid" of God in a fearful sense of the word, but we need to realize how powerful and mighty He is. In Revelation 1:17–18, the apostle John recounted, "And when I saw Him, I fell at His feet as dead. But He laid His right hand on me, saying to me, 'Do not be afraid; I am the First and the Last. I am He who lives, and was dead, and behold, I am alive forevermore. Amen.'"

TEACHING OPPORTUNITY

Mission-Minded Object Lesson: Filthy Rags

In Isaiah 64:6 the Bible says, "All our righteous acts are like filthy rags" (NIV). The next time you come across an extremely dirty rag in your house, use it as an opportunity to share an important lesson with your child. We may think our own self-efforts help us earn "Brownie points" with God. But, to Him, our human works are as worthless as stinky rags. If we try to *earn* favor with God—instead of trusting in Jesus—it's like collecting yucky rags. The more they pile up, the more they stink and mildew.

Only by the cleansing sacrifice of Jesus Christ on the cross have we become "righteous" or in "right standing" before God (Romans 5:19; 2 Corinthians 5:21). It is only because of Christ's forgiveness and His righteousness that we can come before God with boldness and authority to intercede on behalf of others. Along with making us righteous, God also commands us to "put on" righteousness as a part of our spiritual armor (Ephesians 6:14). In prayer, each of us must come to God in an attitude of total surrender and humility, keeping our hearts clean and open before Him.

Even a child can pray as a "righteous man" (James 5:16). Continue to remind your child that his or her spirit can be strong and mature, no matter how young he or she may be! When God spoke to young Samuel, He didn't treat Samuel like a little kid, telling him some cute message just to keep him happy. No, God treated Samuel as a "man of God" and revealed to him a hard-hitting message about the high priest of all Israel (1 Samuel 3:10–14).

Q. How can our family pray more effectively?

In order to make an impact for God's kingdom, our prayers need to be effective and accurate. Broad requests, such as "God bless the missionaries" or "Please help poor people to have enough food," are not examples of effective prayer. Instead, our prayers should be specific, knowledgeable, and on target.

TEACHING OPPORTUNITY

Mission-Minded Object Lesson: Bull's-eye Target

Using a target as an illustration, share with your family how God has a plan for our prayers. He doesn't want us just to say any random thing that comes to our mind or to mindlessly ramble (like shooting an arrow any which way). Rather, God wants us to "hit the bull's-eye" in prayer. By finding out more about a situation and by learning from God's Word, we can aim or focus our prayers toward His perfect will.

When you and your child know more about a situation, you can pray more effectively. Through increased understanding, your prayers will be more heartfelt, and you can intercede with more authority and boldness. Learn as much information as you can about the people or situations you are praying for. If you are praying for a missionary family, read their newsletters or research current world events affecting them. If you are praying for a particular nation, look for information in *Operation World*, at the library, or on the Internet. If you are interceding for a group of people, look on the Internet (for example, www.joshuaproject.net) for specific details about their beliefs, and pray against specific strongholds keeping these people in bondage.

Effective prayer is also biblically accurate. We need to search the Scriptures for God's will and seek His direction on how to pray. How can we know the difference between God's will and our own desires? Hebrews 4:12 tells us, "The word of God is living and powerful, and sharper than any two-edged sword, piercing even to the division of soul and spirit, and of joints and marrow, and is a discerner of the thoughts and intents of the heart." And as we learn more about God's heart and His desires, we'll find that our thoughts and prayers will increasingly line up with His will.

Q. How can we pray with more fervency?

God desires our prayers to be fervent and intense. One definition of *fervent* includes the phrase "hot and boiling over"!

🎓 TEACHING OPPORTUNITY

Mission-Minded Object Lesson: Boiling Water

The next time your child is in the kitchen while you're boiling water, talk about how God wants our prayers to be fervent, or "boiling hot," for Him. As you watch the water boil, explain how our prayers can become more effective as they grow in fervency. Sometimes a prayer can become "hot" immediately, but other times it takes a while for a prayer to become intense and effective.

Our prayers need to be hot for God! We need to pray with all of our heart, soul, mind, and strength. If you pray for the lost, pray as if these individuals are depending on your prayers and you are the only one praying for them. It could be that their souls *do* depend on your prayers, and it *may be* that you are the only one interceding on their behalf.

Fervent Prayer in Africa

On my first mission trip to Africa, I was amazed at the fervent prayers of the Ugandan believers on our ministry team. Everyone usually prayed aloud at the same time, as different individuals led along different themes. Some were kneeling or sitting, others were standing, and a few were even lying on the ground. There was a combination of loud prayer and praise as we interceded for a mighty harvest.

Fervent Prayer in South Korea

In Seoul, South Korea, I had the exciting opportunity to attend a Sunday service at the world's largest church, which is led by Pastor Yonggi Cho. I was surprised how much of the service was devoted exclusively to prayer. The huge building practically shook as thousands of Korean believers prayed intently for their nation and the world. Everyone shouted and prayed so fervently that the leader had to ring a bell to get everyone to stop. It was awesome!

Fervent Prayer Is Intense (Not Just Loud!)

Praying with fervency doesn't necessarily mean just praying with a loud volume. In 1 Kings 18, Elijah and the prophets of Baal both prayed for fire to consume a sacrifice. The prophets of Baal cried loudly for hours. Their prayers were noisy and fleshly, yet worthless. Elijah, however, prayed a simple prayer to God with intensity and authority. If we want our prayers to avail much (James 5:16), we must pray with true Spirit-led fervency.

🌐 TEACHING OPPORTUNITY

A Mission-Minded Prayer List

Create a prayer list that your family can use together. Through intercession we can "stand in the gap" for:

- Individuals

Family members	Friends
Unsaved loved ones	Church leaders
Government leaders	Unreached people

- Ministries/Organizations

Our church	Ministries
Schools	Missionary outreaches

- Geographic areas

Our city	Our state, province, or region
Our nation	Other nations

💡 TEACHING OPPORTUNITY

Two Strategies of Intercession: Offensive and Defensive

In most sports it is important to have an offensive and a defensive strategy, and this principle is true for effective intercession. Encourage your family to think about a sport (such as soccer, football, or basketball) that requires both an offense and a defense. Refer to the sports positions (such as forwards, defenders, or goalie), and discuss how these relate to interceding effectively—both offensively and defensively—for God's will to be done.

- **Defensive Intercession:** When there is an emergency—a financial crisis, sickness, or some other trouble—we come against our "opponent" and pray defensively. Yet it's important to remember that we can't win with only a defensive plan!

- **Offensive Intercession:** We shouldn't just wait around to focus our prayers on major problems in our lives or church. Instead, we need to pray offensively. We can follow the Lord's leading and focus on whatever the Holy Spirit wants us to pray about!

Intercession includes a twofold strategy. First, there must be a defensive plan: to come against—or bind—the opponent and his works. Second, there must be an offensive plan: to pray for the power of God to flow—to be loosed—in God's opposite work (see Matthew 18:18). For instance, if you pray for a geographical area where there has been hatred and war, ask God to bind the hatred and loose His love and forgiveness. As your child prays, encourage his or her focus to be on God, not on the devil.

Mission-Minded Object Lesson: Ropes

Write the words "God's Plan" and "Devil's Plan" on two pieces of paper, and tape each paper to the front of two people. Wrap a rope around the person with the "God's Plan" paper. Demonstrate how our prayers of intercession can have two purposes. We "bind" the plans of our enemy. (Take a rope and wrap it around the person with the "Devil's Plan" paper, illustrating how prayer can help to stop bad things.) We also "loose" the plans of God. (Remove the rope around the person with the "God's Plan" paper so that he or she is free, illustrating how prayer can help release good things to happen.)

Our prayers should exalt Jesus Christ and His plans and purposes. Through our fervent intercession, God will show us His mission strategies. Pray for laborers to be thrust into the harvest fields (Luke 10:2)! Pray for open doors to preach the gospel! Pray for boldness in witnessing, and seek God for your part in His global plan.

Recognizing Opposites—
Praying against Evil and for God's Purposes

When teaching your family about prayer and intercession, it is important to recognize the works of the enemy and to know how to pray for God's will in that circumstance. When there is sin, we bind the enemy's works and then ask God to release His opposite works. The following are examples of these opposing works:

When there is sin, we can bind the enemy's works of:	We can pray for God to release His "opposite" work of:
Anger	Gentleness
Confusion	Peace, wisdom
Cursing	God's blessing
Death, murder, suicide	God's life
Despair	God's hope
Discouragement	Encouragement
Division	Unity in Christ
Fear	Faith
Hatred	Love, reconciliation
Independence	Dependence on God
Lust, impurity, bad thoughts	God's love, purity
Poverty	Provision
Prejudice	Unconditional love
Pride	Humility
Religious bondage	Spiritual freedom
Selfishness	Generosity
Self-righteousness	Righteousness in Christ
Sickness, disease	Health, God's healing
Spiritual rebellion	Submission to God

Prayer Stops the Plans of Terrorists

In Kampala, Uganda, a group of African widows live in the meeting place of a church with which we often work. These women live very simply, with only a small mat on the dirt floor. Their sole purpose in life is to intercede. They pray for many hours every day, and during a special mission outreach they often intercede around the clock.

During one outreach, these women "knew" (in prayer) that we were in danger and began to fast and fervently pray for our protection. As they interceded, one of the women saw in a vision our entire ministry team encircled by angels. These prayer partners were able to get a message of warning through to us. That day in the Tanzanian city where we were preaching, local police caught four Islamic terrorists attempting to plant a bomb on the ministry outreach grounds. Our lives had been spared through intercession and a word of warning from our partners.

Q. Are all Christians called to intercession?

All Christians—including children—are called to pray. We are also called to intercede, as the Lord leads, for regular intercession commitments, as a personal intercessor (or prayer partner), in an emergency, or for a geographical area.

"Regular" Intercession

🌐 TEACHING OPPORTUNITY

Weekly Prayer List—
Pray for a Major Area of Society Each Day

You may want to make a list of regular, or ongoing, prayer commitments, which can include family members, your church, missionaries you support, school leaders, government leaders, and other people you are specifically praying for. In YWAM's daily prayer diary, regular responsibilities include prayer for the following seven areas of society, one area each day.

Weekly Prayer List

- Sunday: church and religion
- Monday: family and the home
- Tuesday: the media
- Wednesday: government

- Thursday: education
- Friday: business and commerce
- Saturday: arts and entertainment

Visual Prayer Reminders

Kids often relate better to pictures than to a prayer list. One idea is to have your child make a photo prayer-collage on a bulletin board, on poster board, or in a mini-album. My boys, Mark and Philip (ages ten and six), simply use pushpins to tack photos of all kinds of prayer needs around their beds. These pictures remind them as they drift off to sleep to pray for children in an African village, specific missionaries, and special friends. Encourage your children to be flexible and sensitive to the Holy Spirit as they pray. It is good to have a regular prayer plan, but it's even better to be open to *God's* plans.

"Prayer Partner" Intercession

God raises up people to be prayer partners for individuals, churches, or ministries. Through the years, my husband and I have been grateful for the people—including the children—God has called to faithfully intercede for our ministry and our family.

A Young Prayer Partner's Creative Idea

We heard about a little boy who made a wristband with our family's name on it in order to remind him to pray for us and the mission work we do. We were humbled and blessed by his prayer partnership with us.

Encouragement from a Prayer Partner

One precious friend has been a personal intercessor for our ministry for over sixteen years. This woman has called at times to share a word of encouragement, which has always been timely.

Once, when I was discouraged and unsure about going on a particular mission trip to Jamaica, she felt led to call and encourage me to go. As we spoke on the phone, she shared two words that she felt the Lord had given her in prayer for me. The two words were "No resistance!"

Because of her encouragement, I decided to go—and the outreach was a total success! Throughout the trip, our family met *no resistance* to our ministry. We were encouraged, and God opened many doors! We preached on streets and in churches and even shared the gospel in public schools across the country. Not one principal turned us down for an assembly, and over five thousand people surrendered their lives to Jesus Christ!

"Emergency" Intercession

As you grow in intercessory prayer, you (or even your child) may wake up in the night with an urge to pray for someone. Or you may be about your daily routine when you suddenly think of a particular person or need. When this happens, be aware that God may be using you to intercede for a crisis.

1. *Be on call for prayer.* We may never know the impact of our prayers, but we should always be "on call" for emergencies. And as one person in our family is feeling this need to pray, we can all agree together.

2. *Be instant in prayer.* When God gives a "strong thought" about someone or a sudden burden to pray, we need to pray! When this feeling of urgency comes, pray as soon as possible and continue praying until the heaviness leaves.

3. *Be obedient in prayer.* Pray hard, as if your prayers will make a difference between life and death—because, at times, it *is* this important!

Emergency Intercession for Our Lost Son

Years ago, when our children were young, my husband and his parents were fishing at a nearby river with two of our boys when they suddenly realized that our five-year-old son, Patrick, was missing.

Desperately, Jon ran up and down the river, looking for Patrick. The river turned into fierce rapids not far downstream, and he feared Patrick could have fallen into the water.

During his search along the riverbank, Jon met several young fishermen who were relaxing and enjoying their day. "Please," Jon yelled, "have you seen a little blond-haired boy? He's lost and may have fallen into the river!"

Not one of these men seemed to care. It wasn't their problem. They didn't want to be bothered—and they just kept fishing.

Jon continued to search, and eventually several police officers joined in to help. A helicopter patrol scanned the river; but even after hours of frantic searching, no one could find our son . . .

That afternoon, across the country, a longtime friend of mine and her three children were sitting on the floor, folding laundry. I had not seen this woman since college, and I hadn't even spoken with her for several years. Yet she suddenly felt a tremendous burden to pray. As she started to pray, the Lord directed her prayers toward our son, Patrick! In the midst of little kids and unfolded clothes, she interceded for him fervently. She felt that he was lost, so she began to intercede specifically for Jon to find him. She prayed for me to have peace and for God to lead us to Patrick . . .

Back at the river, a man on a mountain bike came to Jon and said, "I haven't seen your kid, but I think I know where he is."

A while later, this man returned with little Patrick on his shoulders! The man told us that the night before he dreamed of finding a little blond boy on a certain mountain trail. When the man heard about the search, he immediately went to that trail. Sure enough, there was our son (alone, yet unhurt, other than some scrapes and scratches). Patrick had wandered up a steep cliff and had strayed over a mile away.

That day, we experienced firsthand the power of God—released through emergency intercession.

We also learned a vital lesson about how it feels to be a parent urgently searching for a lost child. How our heavenly Father's heart must break for the lost! He sees His children in sin! He knows the situation is urgent! He knows it's a matter of eternal life and death. Yet how many of us sit back in complacency, not wanting to be bothered? How often do we respond like those selfish fishermen by the river? May we have His heart of compassion!

Protected through Emergency Intercession

One of my first experiences of God's protection through others' prayers happened when I was sixteen years old. One afternoon a girlfriend and I were walking on a back street of a major US city. Suddenly a rough-looking street gang approached us, and we felt helpless as these young men surrounded us and began to harass and slap us. We were all alone with no one near.

At the very same time, however, my parents were hosting a prayer meeting at our house with several family friends. They had committed the entire day to prayer and fasting. Suddenly a woman in the group felt a tremendous burden to pray for the protection of their children. In unity, the entire group prayed earnestly for God to surround each of their children with angels and supernatural protection . . .

Also at the same time, a close teenage friend of mine (a missionary's daughter, by the way!) suddenly thought about me. She started praying, and in her mind she began to "see" a picture of me walking down a street. Then suddenly, in her vision, a circle of darkness surrounded me. My friend continued praying fervently until she "saw" a bright light shine in the center of the circle; then suddenly the darkness left.

From my perspective, this street gang—for no apparent reason—suddenly turned and ran away. My friend and I immediately ran to her house and, together with her parents, called the police to report the incident.

A few months later, I had to testify in court against these men. We learned that this street gang had been arrested for attacking and raping several girls. When the judge asked them why they ran away from my friend and me so suddenly, they had no answer; they just felt they had to "get out of there fast"!

I knew that God intervened because people were praying.

Fleeing Rwanda

Many of our prayer partners felt a heavy burden to pray as my husband was ministering in Rwanda in 1994, shortly after the terrible Rwandan genocide.

Early one morning, on the day of a planned outreach in the city of Gitarama, Jon had a dream of Joseph and Mary escaping to Egypt with baby Jesus (which he said was as clear as if he were watching a Bible video). He then "saw" in his dream the outreach grounds where they planned to preach that evening. In his dream, he saw the crowd attacked in a massive slaughter; and he, along with six other team members, felt God's direction to *Get out of the country—now!*

The team packed and left immediately, escaping across the border just before it was closed. Within hours after their departure, war broke out in that very city of Gitarama, and over seven thousand people were killed.

We were so thankful for God's protection through prayer!

"Area" Intercession

Sometimes God wants us to intercede for a specific geographical area, such as a city, nation, or region of the world. In Genesis 18, Abraham interceded for Sodom and Gomorrah, and in Psalm 122:6 we are encouraged to "pray for the peace of Jerusalem." Ephesians 6:12 states that "we do not wrestle against flesh and blood, but against principalities, against powers, against the rulers of the darkness of this age, against spiritual hosts of wickedness in the heavenly places."

Four Examples of Area Intercession

- *A prayer journey to Bhutan*: Some friends of mine traveled to Bhutan (as tourists) for a "prayer journey." Their purpose was to intercede at specific key locations throughout this central Asian country. I wondered, at first, if this was a waste of ministry resources. But only a few months later, political laws changed to allow foreign missionaries to enter the country!

- *Praying corporately for peace in an African city*: My husband and several other ministers with Harvest Ministry traveled to Kitgum, Uganda, on the border of Sudan—a remote city filled with refugees. For nearly thirty years this area has been devastated by war and paralyzed by the fear of rebel soldiers. Approximately forty thousand people gathered each night of the outreach to hear the Good News of Jesus; and this massive crowd prayed, corporately and fervently, for peace. One evening, many people had a strong sense that something "broke" in the spiritual dimension. One week later the news reported an official cease-fire in the war in Southern Sudan. Some may think it was just a "coincidence," but we choose to believe it was one of those "God-incidences" that happen when believers pray!

- *Praying in Washington DC*: When I spent a few days in Washington DC, I took time to pray for the United States. I visited the National Cathedral and spent time prayer-walking around the grounds and throughout this beautiful place that was built to honor Jesus Christ. I prayed for God's grace over this country. As an American citizen, I repented on behalf of my nation and asked God to forgive the sins of my country. As I visited the US Supreme Court Building, I prayed for the judicial courts of this land and interceded for evil laws, such as legalized abortion, to be changed. Throughout my tours I prayed for God to have mercy (God's favor that we don't deserve) on our land, despite our great faults. My location may not have made a difference to God, but being in those places definitely helped me to pray with increased fervency and passion.

- *Prayer-walking a neighborhood*: In a nearby city, a local church organized a summer of prayer-walking its community. The pastor told us how encouraged and surprised he has been by the positive response and cooperation from the congregation. At least once a week, one to three individuals walk and pray through every street of their city, including the business district, praying for blessing, for a softening of people's hearts, and for wisdom in evangelism. The leader of this outreach walked through her neighborhood and noticed many unkempt yards and overgrown weeds. She asked, *Lord, is there a spirit of oppression over this neighborhood?* Then she specifically prayed against it. The following week, many of these same yards were mowed and cleaned up. She felt the Lord say to her, *See how prayer is making a difference? And you can't even see all that's happening in the spiritual dimension!*

Daniel 10:10–13 gives us a glimpse into the effect of prayer over particular areas. In this passage, an angel is sent because of Daniel's prayers, yet for twenty-one days the evil prince of the kingdom of Persia withstands him in the heavenly realm. As Daniel continues to pray, another angel, the chief prince Michael, is sent to help, and finally the victory is won.

Throughout the earth, a spiritual battle is taking place; and it is not a game! For God's will to be achieved, we need to pray and intercede with accuracy and fervency. We need to emphasize to our children that the battle is not in the flesh but in the spirit. Second Corinthians 10:4 tells us, "The weapons of our warfare are not carnal but mighty in God for pulling down strongholds."

God has defeated the devil through the cross of Calvary and the resurrection of Jesus Christ. At the same time, a quick glance at our world's current situation definitely reveals that the devil still has quite a bit of authority and power. In Ephesians 2:2 the enemy is called "the prince of the power of the air." His strongholds can be through belief systems (such as Hinduism or atheism) or through major sins of a particular area (such as a people group bound by witchcraft or immorality). The devil can also have strongholds in individual lives through fear, depression, anger, hatred, or addictions. As Christians, we must realize that God has delegated His authority to us—as people in His kingdom who are living on this earth and made righteous through Christ—to "pull down" these strongholds through prayer.

A PRAYER ROOM IN INDIA

By Cassie Diacogiannis

Our "prayer room" was set up with cushions on the floor, pictures and maps on the walls, and soft music playing in the background. Every area of the room was focused on praying for different nations, people groups, or mission needs. Crayons and markers lined the edge of the floor so that children could write their prayers on the paper-covered wall.

"All right, kids, when we go into our prayer room, remember that we're not playing around but praying and being serious."

I knew these seventy-five kids understood what I was saying, but I wasn't sure how they would respond. This mission outreach in India had been full of surprises, but I couldn't have prepared myself for what happened next.

The children and I were part of the Western India YWAM Family Conference in the city of Lonavala, India; and I was responsible for teaching all the "YWAMer" kids while their parents were having intense times of networking and conference sessions. When our YWAM base leader gave me permission to bring all the children into the prayer room during the sessions, I jumped at the opportunity. I knew it would be powerful to see missionary kids from around the globe praying for the world. And I couldn't have been more blessed by what I witnessed.

As the kids entered the room, they took off their shoes and lined them up in rows. As they quietly entered this place of worship, the older children helped the younger ones remember why we were there. A moment later, as I walked into the room, it's hard to explain what I saw. The room was filled with seventy-five praying children, all of them under twelve years old. The children were praying for the United States, Pakistan, Iraq, many other nations, and YWAM bases around the world. Some prayed loudly, some prayed silently, and others were worshiping with their hands lifted high to Jesus. A few were sitting quietly on the red cushions and simply watching. But all were very seriously focused on the Lord.

As I walked over to the "wailing wall," the area set aside for specific prayer requests, I saw that a little boy had written the word *Antarctica* in his best penmanship. He had his hand near the word and was praying softly in a strange language. As I came near, he explained that he was praying for the scientists there to see the beauty of God's creation so that they would know Him. A few moments later, a seven-year-old girl named Samaya asked if we could pray for a little boy who was missing his mamma. Before I had barely said, "All right, . . ." Samaya had gathered many children to pray for this little boy who had been crying and had not wanted to stay in class. These children put their little hands on the sad boy and started praying in English, Hindi, and other languages.

Whether it was praying for the nations or for one of our own little children, we knew that God was hearing our prayers. The next day, the boy kissed his momma as he was dropped off and bounded into class. He was ready to play and to pray with the children who had prayed with him the night before.

> "Will you share your tears for the souls of the nations?"
>
> WENDI STRANZ

— 👥 FROM MY CHILDREN'S PERSPECTIVE —

HELL IS REAL!

By Joshua Dunagan, at age eight

One night when I was eight years old, I was sitting in our living room, thinking about my dad. He was away on a missionary trip to Africa, and I started praying for him. As I prayed, the Lord showed me something. I began thinking about all the people in the world who don't know Jesus and how my dad was sharing the gospel at that very moment. Suddenly, it hit me how people who don't know Jesus can't go to heaven . . . they go to hell.

I kept praying and began to realize how terrible hell really is and how people in hell are stuck there—forever!

It's hard to explain what happened, but God did something inside me. I began to cry, for a long time, and it changed the way I thought about the lost. I realized that I had never led anyone to the Lord, and I prayed specifically that God would give me a chance to share with someone that week.

Afterward, I wrote this letter:

> Dear God, I love you so much. Please let me have a chance to share the gospel with someone this week. Lord, you are precious to me.
>
> From Joshua

Dear God
I love you so Much
please let me have
a canc to cher the Gosple
With somyon
this week.
Lord you ar
presis to me
From Joshua

(Note: Later that week, Joshua went to a park and shared the gospel with a young boy named Randy, and then Joshua prayed with him to receive Jesus. Within two years, at the young age of ten, Joshua himself was boldly preaching in Africa—about Jesus and about the fire of Elijah—to intent crowds of over ten thousand people!)

— 👫 FROM MY CHILDREN'S PERSPECTIVE —

WE LOVE TO PRAY!

Mark (age eleven): "I think it's really important to pray! I like to go on prayer-walks outside, and I even made a special 'prayer place' out in the woods. One time I made a prayer closet in my room, and other times I simply put pictures on my bedroom wall. I like to pray for my African prayer partner (his name is Moses) and special friends and missionaries who live in other countries."

Caela Rose (age nine): "When I pray, I know that I'm really talking to God, not to myself. Sometimes God has even helped me to pray and fast (where I didn't eat anything, other than juice and water, for a whole day). No one made me do this, but after our pastor taught about the importance of prayer and fasting, I really felt that God wanted me to do it. Even though I was very hungry, fasting encouraged me to pray harder, and it really drew me closer to God."

Philip (age six): "I'm just six years old, but I like to pray too! I like to worship at church, and sometimes I go to church prayer (even if it's mostly just grownups). I even like to make up songs (good songs) to Jesus. I also like to pray for my special friend, Ivan, in Africa. And I love Jesus!"

Ten Prayer Projects

1. Take a prayer-walk around your neighborhood, quietly praying for each neighbor as you walk by.

2. Have each child pick a neighbor and take that person a small gift—such as flowers, cookies, or a homemade card that says something like "I'm glad you're my neighbor." Pray beforehand for God to prepare the way and soften your neighbor's heart. Encourage your child to mention that he or she has been praying for them and to ask if they have any special prayer needs.

3. Create a map of your country. As each state, province, or region is added, have your child pray specifically for that area.

4. Purchase a simple world map to display on a wall, and add a bundle of dried wheat above it (or display a bundle of wheat in your kitchen as a decoration) to remind you to pray for a great harvest of souls around the world.

5. Add a "10/40 Window" to your world map. Use colored yarn and pushpins or colored tape to highlight this important area of the world where there are so many unreached people who need Jesus. Make horizontal lines along the latitude lines 10 degrees and 40 degrees north of the equator. Make vertical lines to include all of Africa to the west and all of Asia to the east. Pray for this area.

6. Toss an inflatable globe around the room while playing music, as in musical chairs. When the music stops, the person holding the globe prays for the specific place where his or her fingers are touching.

7. Have your child make a "Ten Most Wanted" list or poster. Have them think of ten people who need Jesus. These can be relatives, friends, neighbors, famous people, or the man

who works at the convenience store. Use this list or poster to remind you to pray for these people to come to know the Lord.

8. Use the acronym THUMB to remember the five major segments of people who need Jesus: T for Tribal, H for Hindu, U for Unreligious, M for Muslim, and B for Buddhist.

9. Using your church directory, talk about all the ministries and jobs in your church. Relate each person to a part of a body and how every part is important. Pray for these various individuals, including your pastor, and for the people in your congregation as a whole.

10. Simply pray!!

CHAPTER 7

Missions and Family Finances

"For where your treasure is, there your heart will be also."

JESUS CHRIST (MATTHEW 6:21)

How your family views money and possessions is intrinsically connected with how you view God's priorities in life. As Christians, we should have the perspective that everything belongs to God: all of our time, all of our talents, all of our life decisions, and, yes, all of our money. I believe it is important to teach our children about God's principle of tithing (giving 10 percent of our income to Him), but even more importantly we need to instill in our family that 100 percent of absolutely everything in our lives belongs to God. This principle is much easier *caught*—by our example—than *taught* by our words.

Every Christian family should live by faith. It doesn't matter if you are called to a conventional occupation or called to be a pastor or a missionary; in actuality, every believer is called to "full-time ministry." Every believer is called to serve the Lord as His ambassador, in whatever area that might be. There is a special grace, a high accountability before God, and many unique challenges for believers who commit to earning their entire livelihood by the gospel; but every mission-minded follower of God should live by faith. Often the most difficult challenge to accepting God's calling to ministry or missionary work is the question of money and trusting in God's provision, especially provision for an entire family.

Nobody wants to be a missionary mooch or a religious bum. The very fact that we have these fears reveals a struggle in our core attitudes about work, faith, and God's provision.

This chapter is written for two purposes. First, I want to encourage each family that is called to forgo a traditional salary or occupation (or that may be called to do so in the future) to obey God's call into ministry or missionary work. Even a traditional pastoral position or an appointment on a church staff seems more stable than a mission-oriented occupation or a ministry with an evangelistic or outreach focus. Lost people don't buy tickets (or pay their tithes) to hear the gospel. But they need to hear, and someone has to be willing to reach out to them. Second, this chapter is written to encourage every mission-minded family to understand the tremendous needs concerning world missions and international evangelism. Every one of us (including pastors, laypeople, and even missionaries) needs to support God's work generously.

The Little Blue Lamp

My husband and I were both twenty-one years old and had just completed Bible school and university education when the Lord began training us to rely totally on Him. We were living in Oklahoma and preparing to move over two thousand miles away, to Oregon, to step into full-time ministry.

Because of prayer, we felt God calling us to mission evangelism and specifically (in our situation) that Jon was not to work any job for pay, outside of the ministry. We had accumulated a modest savings and were beginning to sell our belongings. But no matter how many times we tried to calculate our future budget, there was no way, financially speaking, that it would work. Even if all of our things sold for top dollar, we realized there would be nothing to live on beyond the first few months.

We didn't have a support base. We didn't know anyone in the city where we were headed. And the more we thought about it and tried to crunch the numbers, the more concerned and frustrated we became.

As graduation day drew near, Jon earnestly began to seek the Lord for direction and provision. One day, after a time of fervent prayer, Jon came in and told me, "Hon, you'd better sit down." My husband then proceeded to unload what could have been a bomb for a young wife: "Ann, I believe God wants us to forsake everything and totally depend on Him, not on ourselves. Just as the disciples left their full nets to follow Jesus, I believe God wants us to give away everything—our car, our savings, and everything we've had for sale."

For a moment, I let the words sink in. It sounded crazy, but somehow God instantly confirmed Jon's words in my heart.

It wasn't because of something he and I had heard before. We weren't mimicking someone else's testimony. (And we're not suggesting anyone else try this at home!) Yet somehow, deep inside, we both felt this was indeed what God wanted for us. Besides, if Jon's idea *was* from God (which I felt it was), I knew it would work; and if it *wasn't* from God, we shouldn't be in ministry! A faith came that was unexplainable. All worry and anxiety left, and we were instantly filled with excitement.

That night, we called a few friends and told them to come and take anything they wanted. The next day, we gave our car to a fellow student who had wanted to buy it. In the next church service, we gave our entire savings in the offering. We gave a beautiful hand-carved baby crib to a woman I had prayed with (who, by the way, had been barren, but was now expecting!). And most difficult of all, I presented our church's worship director with a treasured silver flute my parents had sacrificed to buy for my sixteenth birthday.

Now there was no possible way we could step out in ministry on our own. If it worked, it would have to be the Lord's provision. And we just knew He would provide!

But two days before we were to move, reality suddenly hit. We had nothing. The lease was up on our apartment. Our church had already prayed for us and sent us out. We had no vehicle and no money. How would we live? How were we going to get across the country? Could we really expect someone to give us a car within the next few days? It seemed impossible.

Jon looked over at me, sitting on the floor with our newborn, as he suddenly felt a wave of despair, responsibility, and condemnation.

He desperately cried out to the Lord, "God, did I hear You right?"

As he prayed, Jon felt a reassuring peace and a still, small voice: *Yes, and as soon as you do everything I have told you to do, you will see My provision.*

Jon kept asking me all morning if there was something we had not yet done, but we couldn't think of anything. Finally, we got out our "for sale" list and went down the items one by one—until we came to . . .

Blue Lamp—$5

Looking across the room, we saw the little blue lamp sitting on a cardboard box in the corner. We had found it (then an ugly orange) at a garage sale, brought it home, and painted it country blue.

"The lamp! The lamp!" we both shouted. "We forgot to give away the lamp!"

Immediately, Jon grabbed that little blue lamp (along with a handful of pots and pans) and headed to our neighbor's apartment. Our young bachelor friend didn't know what to think when Jon loaded his arms with the strange combination, saying, "Here—God wants you to have these!"

Jon hurried back to our apartment, and within three minutes (that is no exaggeration!) we received a phone call from a man we barely knew.

"Is this Jon Dunagan?"

"Yes."

"Do you need a car?"

Jon attempted to conceal his growing excitement. "Well . . . uh, why do you ask?"

"Well, my wife and I have been feeling that God wants us to give you our car. We've never done anything like this before, so we prayed about it all last night. It wasn't until just a few minutes ago that we finally felt a peace about calling you."

That last step of obedience—giving away that insignificant blue lamp—released God's provision! Before, we trusted in ourselves and our stuff, but now we depended on God.

Within two days, we left for Oregon—arriving in town with our little car, a few dishes (which weren't on our "for sale" list), some clothes, one baby, and only twenty-seven dollars!

We preached in parks and witnessed on the streets; and a roller-skating rink allowed us to use their building—*free of charge*—for weekly services. We even found a nice fourplex with an amazing move-in special: "Move in today . . . and don't pay for three months"!

Our First Mission Trip

After we had been in Oregon a short time, God led us to a pastor who helped arrange our first overseas mission trip: to Hong Kong, Macao, China, and the Philippines. The Lord supernaturally provided money for our airline tickets, but when it came time to leave, we had no money for traveling expenses—not even one dollar to buy gas to get to the airport!

Here we were, a young couple with an eighteen-month-old baby, and I was seven months pregnant. Our only overseas contacts were complete strangers, and we didn't know if we needed to pay our expenses once we were there.

How could we leave with no money? Would we be a blessing or a burden? Was this really God's will?

As we prayed together, God again gave us peace that comes only from Him. He gave us a tremendous burden for the lost in those countries and reassured us that He could provide there just as easily as He could provide in America. For Him, there was no difference; but for us, it was a lesson in trust.

We decided to pack our car and drive toward the airport until our near-empty gas tank ran dry. Right before we left, we made a last-minute check through our apartment and noticed a new message on our answering machine: "Hey, Jon and Ann, if you haven't left yet, I've got something for you down at the church . . ."

That "something" was a twenty-dollar bill—just enough to get us to the airport! On our way overseas, the Lord opened up an opportunity for us to share with a small college group at a church in Maui, Hawaii. We were completely surprised when they offered to take a special missions offering for our trip! These people blessed us and sent us on our way.

Throughout the several-month outreach, no one knew of our meager financial situation. Every step along the way we had enough money to pay for every expense. We were able to bless our ministry contacts monetarily. And we even came home with souvenirs! We saw firsthand the "ripe harvest" overseas, and our lives and ministry have never been the same.

Continuing to Trust God

For over twenty years, my husband and I have not worked a job—for pay—outside of the ministry; and we have never "itinerated" to raise ministry funds (although we realize that many, in fact most, missionaries are led by the Lord to do this). We have simply trusted God. And He has faithfully provided for hundreds of international outreaches and for every need for our growing family.

When we have a financial need, we seek God's direction. Sometimes we share a ministry need in our monthly newsletter (which we only send to those who have requested it). Sometimes we tell no one and simply pray. Other times the Lord directs us to mention something to a particular person. Sometimes He directs us to give generously to someone else. We often practice "tithing in advance" (just as people gave of their "firstfruits" in the Bible): we give 10 percent of what we need for an outreach before any money comes in.

No matter how the details work out, God consistently comes through! Over the years, He has provided for missionary motorcycles and village church buildings, as well as for college tuition and orthodontic braces for our children.

God's provision doesn't always look the same, but it's always there. One time we trusted God for over fifteen thousand dollars for an African outreach; then, soon afterward, we trusted God for us to go back to Africa without even one penny—using a free airline ticket! God's provision was met in a supernatural way for each trip, but the provision came quite differently.

When another "impossible" situation comes, the Lord simply reminds us how we began; and He continually reassures us that He will keep meeting our needs today . . . and tomorrow.

How Does a Missionary Raise Support?

When beginning full-time missionary work, one of the first steps a person will take—while praying and seeking the Lord's will—is to build a support base for prayer, mutual encouragement, and financial partnership. As Betty Barnett of YWAM has written in her excellent book, *Friend Raising: Building a Missionary Support Team That Lasts*, this is a process of raising friends, not funds.

It is important for mission-minded families to do their best to understand the challenging steps new missionaries must take to reach the ministry goal God is calling them to make. As we take time to consider a missionary's initial (and ongoing) challenge to trust God for financial provision, it can help us to be more empathetic and encouraging. Missionaries need constant encouragement—in prayer, friendship, and finances—to see God's visions fulfilled. Even simple comments, such as "I just got your newsletter in the mail, and I'm so proud of you!" or "Hey, I want you to know that I'm praying for people to give toward your ministry!" can make a huge impact.

🌐 TEACHING OPPORTUNITY

Learn How a Missionary Builds a Support Team

Even if your family is not called to full-time missionary service, look at each step a new missionary has to face and consider how your mission-minded family could be a support, help, and encouragement to new missionaries.

- A new missionary usually begins by seeking counsel from a pastor or a mission organization. (Your family could pray with them for God's wisdom.)

- As God leads, the new missionary usually hopes to share the new vision at his or her home church or at a church of close friends or family members. (You could mention this opportunity to your pastor or church leaders.)

- Sometimes a table display needs to be assembled with photos of the people or a map of the projected area. (Your family could stand by their display or, if you're computer savvy, help make a DVD or PowerPoint presentation.)

- It is usually helpful to have a ministry brochure available. This brochure often includes photos, a brief introduction of the missionary and his or her family, a description of previous ministry experiences, and the missionary's vision for the future. (Your family can give encouraging comments or help with mailing.)

- A new ministry brochure usually includes a brief recommendation from a pastor and perhaps others and a simple response card. (Your family could collect recommendations and positive comments about the missionary.)

- When sharing a new vision, missionaries try to remember that God is their ultimate source of provision—not any particular people. "Where God guides, He provides!" Without portraying a begging attitude, new missionaries attempt to convey their burning heart for the lost and to share their vision for the future. Many missionaries see tremendous needs that they are unable to meet by themselves; part of their calling is to help convey this need to others. (Your family can help by requesting prayer support for specific missionary needs.)

- Oftentimes, the thought of facing friends and family to raise necessary missionary support is far more terrifying than the thought of facing a tribe of cannibalistic headhunters! It's a great blessing when a new missionary meets someone with an encouraging and compassionate heart. (Your family can be this encouragement!)

- At the conclusion of a new missionary's presentation, it is very helpful if a pastor (or someone other than the missionary) invites people to join with this new missionary in prayer and/or financial support. (Perhaps you can fill that role.)

🌍 TEACHING OPPORTUNITY

Make an Introductory Missionary Brochure

As a family, you could help a new missionary with an introductory brochure, design a brochure for a missionary who needs an updated design, or even write your own family letter to communicate your heart for world missions or to encourage prayer for a specific need.

Imagine you're a new missionary. Follow the steps below to begin communicating with your supporters. (And when you are in the midst of that tedious job of signing and mailing your annual Christmas letter or cards, remember to pray for God's blessing and anointing on your missionaries—who need to communicate with their partners regularly, nearly every month!)

- Begin with an up-to-date family photo, and design an attractive prayer card.

- Ask the Lord who to include in your first mailing. (Missionaries often begin by making a list of relatives, church friends, coworkers, high school and college friends, those on their Christmas list, or people they meet as they share their new ministry vision.)

- What to include in your mailing to supporters: a simple letter, a quality ministry brochure, a return envelope, and a response card (if desired).

- Make your communication personal. If possible, a new missionary should precede the first mailing with a personal contact. A friendly call or a short note simply to touch base with a longtime friend could make a big difference. And when the initial newsletter is sent, it is always good to include a personal, handwritten note.

It is important to realize that stepping into full-time ministry or mission work usually requires dying to self-righteous pride and reevaluating self-sufficient attitudes. Sometimes a person may listen to a missionary and inwardly mutter: *Ugh! There is no way on earth I would take money from people I know. If God ever provided supernaturally, that would be one thing. But if He ever wanted me to be a missionary, I would never be like some tramp—just mooching off friends and family!*

Do we consider "living by faith" equivalent to begging like a homeless vagabond or perpetually surviving on food stamps and welfare? Thoughts like these degrade God's calling and the obedience of His frontline warriors. As mission-minded parents and teachers, it is vital to esteem God's missionaries and the tremendous sacrifices they make. Remember that our children will grasp our attitudes even more than the things we say.

📖 DARING TO LIVE ON THE EDGE

An excerpt from *Daring to Live on the Edge*, by Loren Cunningham

In his excellent book *Daring to Live on the Edge: The Adventure of Faith and Finances*, Loren Cunningham addresses many challenges of stepping into full-time ministry. As the founder and director of YWAM (Youth With A Mission), Cunningham shares from his vast experience and from his heart as he encourages others to walk in obedience to God's calling—whatever that may be.

For many of us, pride blocks us from being the receivers of generous giving. We would rather be self-sufficient. I have often talked with people who wanted to be missionaries some day—when they could pay their own way to go. But the sad fact is that even if you could manage to remain unentangled with debt and find a way to bankroll your own work, you would miss the terrible-but-wonderful humbling heart link that occurs when people put money in your hand, saying the Lord told them to give it to you.

There is a special bond forever between you and the giver. You will care about and pray for the giver in a different way than you pray for those who have never given to you personally. You will also quite naturally want to share news with your giver about your ministry, reporting what the gift has done in the work of the Lord. And prayer will go up on all sides—the spiritual warfare that is necessary for anything to be accomplished. It might not seem possible to struggling missionaries or pastors, but if a giant foundation were to fund their work or some billionaire were to write out a huge check, it could be a death knell for their ministry. Missionaries need much more help than money. We need people backing us up, praying for the extension of God's kingdom, engaging with us in spiritual warfare through their giving and intercession.

The giver is blessed in the process, too. Jesus told us, "Where your treasure is, there your heart will be also" (Matthew 6:21 NIV). When we give our "treasure" to specific people and their ministries, our hearts are there with them. They may be halfway around the world in an area we may never visit—but we are closer to these people and what God is doing in that country because of our giving. This kind of heart link giving allows any Christian from any part of the world to "go out" and help fulfill the Great Commission. And it is God's way of forging and strengthening relationships.

"Though your riches increase,
do not set your heart on them."

PSALM 62:10 (NIV)

A Few (More) Thoughts about Faith and Finances

The next sections are for mission-minded families that are *not* called to be missionaries

Advice from a Mission-Minded Single Mom

Every month I put money aside and work extra jobs to have the means to go when and where the Lord shall direct. I encourage everyone to do what he or she can to save little by little as well. The Lord makes ways when you are working for Him! But it's also important to remember not to be so caught up in saving that we forget to give. (This is a daily reminder that I need to keep giving myself!)

Challenged by Cluttered Closets

With twisted hangers, bulging drawers, and too many clothes, the kids and I began our major closet-cleaning attack. It took days; but as we conquered our last pile, we felt victorious—with sacks for the Dumpster and sacks to give away. Best of all, we finished just in time for me to leave for a short-term mission trip.

I was headed to Uganda and soon was surrounded by orphans with bare bottoms and wearing nothing but rags and ripped-up shirts. I couldn't think of anything but these precious children and my cluttered closets. Then I felt the Lord whisper, *I'm the One naked on these streets!* I immediately went to buy armloads of children's clothing. But the situation turned pathetic: mothers came running from everywhere, holding up naked babies, and begging for help. The need was beyond me; and I tell you, it did something to my heart.

Back home, our family raised funds to clothe that whole village. And this year, we even started an orphanage. The world's needs are huge, but they're not beyond God!

Ten Ways to Raise Money for Missions

There are many ways to raise money for international mission projects. Here is a list of activities commonly used by children's churches, youth groups, and short-term mission teams. The time will come, however, when these efforts won't be enough. A true mission-minded family just needs to earn and save money, managing that money according to what's important.

1. Organize a car wash; rather than charging a set amount, receive donations.

2. Collect newspapers for recycling.

3. Recycle aluminum (and go around neighborhoods to get even more).

4. Use creative offering baskets. The last few weeks at our church, someone held up a big rubber boot to collect money for a mission trip to the Philippines. A missionary wants to buy rubber barn boots and other gifts for pastors in remote villages; the boot was simply a fun way for the church to catch the vision. Another idea is to use African-looking baskets.

5. Track a missions goal on a "thermometer" poster or in the church bulletin.

6. Have a family garage sale.

7. Make and sell something, like crafts or after-church lattes and espressos.

8. Donate a service in exchange for a donation for a mission trip.

9. Collect spare change in special containers, such as a coffee can with pictures related to the mission project and a hole for coins in the lid. I know of a small church in which the kids raised thousands of dollars for missions by doing this.

10. Have a bake sale after church.

A Coast Guard Cutter . . . or a Luxury Liner?

What kind of lifestyle is appropriate for a mission-minded family? Does God want all Christians to subsist just above the poverty line? Is it OK to live in extreme wealth and extravagance? Or does God have a divine balance economically for each family? An interesting perspective is to remember that we are in a spiritual battle, with eternal souls at stake. As mission-minded believers, we should go through life as if we are on a rescue ship, not a luxury craft.

During World War II, the *Queen Mary*, a huge ocean liner, was converted into a troopship. In *Serving as Senders*, Neal Pirolo writes:

> Today the museum aboard the *Queen Mary* affords a stunning contrast between the lifestyles appropriate in peace and war. On one side of a partition, the tables prepared for high society hold a dazzling array of dishes, crystal and silver. On the other side, one metal tray with indentations replaces 15 dishes and saucers. Bunks, eight tiers high, accommodate 15,000 troops in contrast to the 3,000 wealthy patrons in

peacetime transport. To so drastically reconstruct the vessel took a national emergency. The survival of a nation depended upon it. Should you replace your china with metal trays? No! But allow the Holy Spirit to challenge every aspect of your lifestyle.

> "You may say to yourself, 'My power and the strength of my hands have produced this wealth for me.' But remember the LORD your God, for it is he who gives you the ability to produce wealth."
>
> DEUTERONOMY 8:17–18 (NIV)

A Few Startling Financial Facts

- More money is spent each year on chewing gum than on world missions.

- Every fifty-two days more money is spent on pet food than is spent annually on missions.

- The US poverty level is in the top 4 percent of world family income.

— FROM MY CHILDREN'S PERSPECTIVE —

GRANDPA'S REWARD
By Patrick Dunagan, age fifteen

Recently, my grandpa Dunagan died. At the time, Dad was overseas on a mission trip in Africa and was unable to get home in time for the memorial service. I had the sad honor of taking Dad's place (along with my five uncles) as one of Grandpa's pallbearers.

My dad wrote this letter before he left. As it was read at Grandpa's memorial service, it really showed me how a father's life can impact his children for God and for missions and, in turn, impact his grandchildren too!

> Dear Dad,
>
> Well, I am off to Africa again! Lord willing, my team will hold two crusades on this outreach. Months of preparation and planning have gone into this endeavor. I pray that God will honor the labor with multitudes of precious souls coming to know Jesus Christ as their Lord and Savior.
>
> Dad, you and Mom were the first people to plant in me a desire for missions evangelism. For many years you had been faithfully in charge of the missions department at East Olympia Community Church—always making sure that these laborers received their material support and plenty of love and encouragement.
>
> I remember one time in particular, when I was about twelve years old, that a certain missionary from South America had come to visit you at the farm. I knew that at the time your own personal finances were tight. However, I observed how you and Mom wanted to bless this man. You saved a little here and a little there and even sold a cow. When you gave your gift, you gave joyfully and humbly. Little did this man know of the sacrifice behind what you gave . . . and seeing your act of giving stirred something inside of me. I immediately ran to my room and gave the missionary all of my money to help him in his work. I figured that if "missions" was that important to you, it had better be important to me.
>
> Dad, in the event that your body passes away while I am in Africa, I know that your soul and spirit are with Jesus. To

be sure, there is nothing I can do to bring life back into your body now. However, through my labors I trust for salvation to be granted to many. More than likely, I would not be able to make it back in time for your funeral; but in that event, I would like to dedicate the souls that come to Christ on this outreach to you. I trust that the Lord will add them to your reward.

I love you, Dad! Thanks for being such a godly example to follow.

Your son,

Jon

"The question is not how much of my money I give to God, but rather how much of God's money I keep for myself."

R. G. LETOURNEAU

"He had everything, but he possessed nothing. There is the spiritual secret."

A. W. TOZER (SPEAKING OF ABRAHAM OFFERING ISAAC)

Part IV

Our Time to Go!

CHAPTER 8

Mission-Minded
Ministry Ideas

When a family ministers together, the spiritual impact is powerful. I strongly believe that even a child, if properly trained and mature in Christ, can effectively share the gospel of Jesus Christ. The purpose for including your children in ministry or on a mission outreach is not merely for your kids to be cute or for your family to look good.

The purpose is to train each member of your family to participate— even now—in Christ's Great Commission, to share with people who desperately need Him.

You can prepare for particular ministries and mission outreaches as a family, but it's important to guard against pushing a child into a particular ministry calling. Allow God to lead each child; and learn, together as a family, how to follow God.

Focus on the Heart of Ministry
(Four Family Ministry "Rules")

- *God deserves all the glory.* Don't take any glory. If someone gives you a compliment, simply say, "Thank you"; then give the praise to God.

- *God deserves all the attention.* Don't distract others. This principle is reinforced by having an attitude that requires attentiveness in church or anytime anyone is sharing or ministering.

- *We're here to build others up, not to tear others down.* Don't criticize others (including your siblings!).

- *We want to make God look good.* Do your best—for the glory of God!

Q. How can I prepare each family member to share a "testimony"?

If your children have grown up loving the Lord, they may think they don't have a powerful testimony. But in actuality this kind of testimony is best, because it doesn't include wasted years of sin and regret and the negative consequences of being separated from God's purposes (although God can use even those "wasted" years for His glory if a person repents).

A Mission-Minded Testimony

When I was about eleven years old, I was asked to share my Christian testimony in a meeting. Right before my turn, a rough-looking motorcycle biker presented the powerful story of God's grace in his life. This man had done many terrible things and had even served time in prison. But he had radically come to know Jesus Christ and was now zealous for Him.

As I compared my simple story with his, I thought my "testimony" was so boring and uneventful. Yet when I stepped off the platform, that biker came and encouraged me to never downplay the power of God in my life. Then he added, "You know, I'd give anything to have a testimony like yours."

📖 TEACHING OPPORTUNITY

Learn How to Prepare a Powerful Testimony

Encourage each member of your family to consider his or her personal relationship with the Lord and to prepare to share this faith with others effectively.

Questions to answer:

- What was your life like without Jesus?

- Encourage a child who accepted the Lord at a young age to share how it wasn't enough to be born into a Christian family. Every person has to receive Jesus for himself or herself.

- When did you accept Jesus Christ as Lord and Savior?

- How did you come to know Jesus?

- Did someone share or pray with you?

- What does it mean to be "saved"?

- What is it like for you to follow Jesus?

- How has God been real and alive in your life? Has God answered a specific prayer, provided for you, or given you peace during a challenging time?

If you share your testimony in a church:

- How can your life and testimony encourage other believers?

- What ages will be in the audience? How can you encourage them?

If you share your testimony with non-Christians:

- How can your experience with God encourage others to follow Jesus?

- What is the primary belief system or religious background of the people with whom you are sharing? How can you effectively share your faith?

— 👫 FROM MY CHILDREN'S PERSPECTIVE —

COULD YOU IMAGINE WORSHIPING A "GOD" THAT HAS TO BE DUSTED?
By Joshua Dunagan, age fifteen

The smell of incense was strong as my dad and I entered a Buddhist temple in Singapore a few weeks ago. It shocked me to see so many normal-looking people bowing down to such weird-looking idols!

As we stood and quietly watched from the back of the temple, I was so thankful that I didn't have to worship some silent statue. After a couple of minutes, a temple worker walked into the glass case and started dusting off the idols—right in front of everybody! I thought, *How could these people worship a "god" that has to be dusted?*

This mission trip came as a real surprise to me, since I found out only a week ahead of time that I was going. The United States had just declared war on Iraq, so airline tickets were cheap; and we saw it as an opportunity to "go"! Jesus said that in the last days "you will hear of wars and rumors of wars. See that you are not troubled. . . . And this gospel of the kingdom will be preached in all the world as a witness to all the nations, and then the end will come" (Matthew 24:6, 14).

The entire outreach was a great eye opener for me. From witnessing to taxi drivers next to massive Asian skyscrapers to passing out Bibles in a small Malaysian fishing village, I saw for myself that people everywhere need Jesus!

🌐 TEACHING OPPORTUNITY

Learn How to Work Effectively with an Interpreter

If your family takes part in a short-term outreach, you will need to learn how to work effectively with an interpreter. A good interpreter will work with you, not against you, and will translate your message smoothly and accurately. It is a great blessing to have a Christian interpreter, especially one with experience sharing and interpreting the plan of salvation. Often, words we take for granted, such as *sin*, *heaven*, *salvation*, and *forgiveness*, are not familiar to an unbeliever and will be difficult to convey. Even so, over the years our family has had the blessing of leading many of our unsaved interpreters to Jesus Christ!

Q. What are some helpful tips for speaking through an interpreter?

- Speak slowly, clearly, and distinctly.

- Say one complete thought (but *only* one complete thought) at a time. Half of a phrase often cannot be translated because the grammatical structure or verb conjugation in the foreign language may be different. The interpreter will usually need to hear your complete thought before he or she can interpret it.

- Use simple, everyday words. Avoid technical and difficult words.

- Avoid slang and figures of speech. Expressions such as "It's cool to be here!" "I'm so fired up about Jesus!" or "Keep an eye out . . ." usually cannot be translated in a way that makes sense to your audience.

- Avoid words with double meanings or jokes involving a play on words (such as "If you've seen one shopping center, you've seen a mall," or "When the actress saw her first strands of gray hair, she thought she'd dye"). Most often your words won't be funny when interpreted, and the people will just stare at you with a confused look.

- If you will be speaking directly from the Bible, share the specific Scripture verses ahead of time with your interpreter so that he or she can look them up and be prepared to translate them correctly.

- To ensure that people understand what you are saying, pay attention to the response from your audience as you speak. Watch for confused expressions or for responses that are not expected. For example, if the entire crowd laughs when you're trying to be serious, your interpreter likely added something.

- Avoid theological terms. If a non-Christian interprets for you, try to substitute simple words for theological ones. For example, in place of the word *sin* you can substitute "the wrong things we do," and instead of *redemption* you can say, "God helps us to come back to Him." Some words, such as *generation*, *legacy*, *information*, and *technology*, may be difficult to translate. If you will be repeating a theme, discuss this with your interpreter ahead of time in order to avoid problems.

- Encourage your interpreter to have the same enthusiasm you have, perhaps even using the same hand motions. This is especially important when ministering to children.

- Practice! When teaching your child how to work with an interpreter, have him or her say a complete phrase and then repeat the phrase again. To flow smoothly and clearly while speaking through an interpreter is not hard; it just takes practice.

📖 TEACHING OPPORTUNITY

Help Your Family Gain a Passion for Kids' Ministry

Over 35 percent of the world's population is under the age of fifteen, and in developing countries this percentage sometimes reaches 50 percent. Over 85 percent of all Christians receive Christ before the age of eighteen; yet this vital reality of evangelism is often overlooked.

Q. How can we have a successful children's outreach?

- *Encourage your kids to reach kids.* A child or young person is a "perfect-sized missionary" to reach other children for the Lord. It is usually nonthreatening for a child to share with another child.

- *Go to a place where kids gather.* Instead of trying to get a group of children to come to you, have a children's outreach in a place where they already are: crowded neighborhoods, parks, beaches, street corners, schools, recreation centers, or by invitation to a home. (In many countries, schools are open for Christian assemblies for the entire student body.) We shouldn't expect unbelievers to come to church; we must go to them.

- *Let people know you're there.* Play fun children's music or circus-style music. Set up a "party" area with balloons and a simple puppet stage (even a brightly colored sheet held between two people). Enthusiastically invite children—and parents—to come and join you. Use a puppet, balloons, or a clown to catch their attention. (I have been amazed at how easy it is to draw a crowd of children overseas; in a foreign country, a few energetic teenagers could draw a hundred children with merely a handful of balloons.) Begin with a few exciting children's contests (such as balloon blowing or pop drinking), accompanied with prizes, to create an exciting atmosphere.

- *When you've gathered a crowd, share the gospel—with ENERGY!* You may want to begin by holding up a newspaper and asking, "Hey! Have you heard the news?" Then share how you have Good News for them. Use simple object lessons to share the plan of salvation with enthusiasm, energy, boldness, and plain language that enables everyone—children, teens, and adults—to understand God's message of salvation. Pray for God's anointing on His Word and realize that the gospel has power to change people's lives.

- *Give an opportunity for people to respond.* Conclude by bringing people to a point of decision, giving them an opportunity to accept Jesus Christ as their Lord and Savior. You may want to ask everyone to bow their heads in prayer, to raise their hands, and/or to come forward—depending on the situation and the receptivity. Make sure everyone understands what it means to receive God's salvation, and then lead people in a prayer to receive and follow Jesus Christ.

- *Help new believers to grow.* Review the gospel message, and share with new believers what it means to grow as a Christian. If possible, distribute follow-up material, and invite them to a nearby church or home Bible study to be introduced to a local pastor or group of believers.

🌐 TEACHING OPPORTUNITY

Learn Easy and Effective Object Lessons

Jesus often taught by referring to a simple object as He shared an important truth about God's kingdom. He used familiar objects that were readily available (such as coins, lilies, and seeds) or easily imagined (such as a woman mixing yeast into bread dough). The teachings of Jesus were always profound, yet simple enough for even children to understand. The following ideas are some of my favorite objects lessons to use on mission trips in developing countries.

- *The Gospel Colors*
  Explain the gospel message through the color *gold* (God wants everyone to go to heaven); *black* (all have sinned); *red* (only the blood of Jesus can take away our sins); *white* (we need God to purify our hearts through salvation in Jesus); *green* (God wants us to grow as a Christian); and *blue* (as believers, we need to be baptized into God's family). You can use large pieces of material or felt (which are easily folded and packed in a suitcase), colored balloons, or even selected children from the audience wearing clothes with these colors.

- *Dirty and Clean Hands*
  Wet your hands and then rub them in dirt (representing sin). Hold up your dirty hands while you share how all have sinned. Wipe your hands on your clothes (representing trying to get rid of our sin by ourselves), noting how the problem only gets worse. Finally, use water (or white shaving cream) and a red washcloth, and clean your hands. Explain how it is only through the blood sacrifice of Jesus Christ and His forgiveness of our sins that our lives can be made clean.

- *Bible Cover Filled with Garbage*
  Use a zippered Bible cover that has a cross or an obvious Christian symbol on it. Note how this looks very good outwardly; but as you slowly open the cover, the audience will see that it is filled with garbage. State that the garbage represents sin. Using a red washcloth, clean out the Bible cover and insert a Bible. Explain how God does not look merely at outward appearances or "religious" motions, but He looks at the heart. Share about the importance of receiving Jesus Christ.

- *Soap and Wash Bucket*

  Show a dirty cloth, representing our sinful lives. The soap and wash bucket represent our salvation through Jesus Christ. (These objects are easy to find anywhere.) Jesus can take our sinful lives and make them clean and pure.

- *Black Balloon*

  As you blow up a black balloon, share how sin usually starts very small but soon grows and becomes worse. Hold up a small pin and explain how the power of Jesus Christ can destroy the sin in our lives—no matter how large or small that sin is. It may seem like a "little thing" to pray and surrender your life to Jesus Christ, but it can make all the difference in the world and for all of eternity. Then pop the balloon with the pin.

- *Large Green Balloon*

  Point to nearby trees and green plants, and talk about how the color green reminds us of things that grow. Blow up the biggest green balloon you can find as you teach about how to grow as a Christian: through loving God and others, praying to God, reading the Bible, going to church, worshiping, sharing the gospel, etc. When the balloon is at its maximum size, point out how we need to continue to grow in the Lord until the day—although we don't know when—our lives on earth are over and we go to heaven. When you (or your interpreter) say the word *heaven*, let go of the balloon and watch it "fly away" as it deflates!

Teaching Your Family to Use Object Lessons

- What you need: The objects mentioned above.

- What to do: Pray for God to help you use these object lessons to share about Jesus effectively. Demonstrate the object lessons, and then have each family member take a turn to share a short section. (For example, one child could share how "*gold* reminds us that God wants us to go to heaven, where even the streets are like gold!")

- Have your family work together to present one or two of these object lessons. Make sure each person speaks clearly and with enthusiasm.

◉ TEACHING OPPORTUNITY

Learn How to Minister with the *EvangeCube*

One of the most outstanding tools for personal evangelism is called the *EvangeCube*. This simple cube is sometimes referred to as "the *JESUS* film of one-to-one evangelism." If you haven't yet seen this wonderful tool, please look at the online demonstration at www.e3resources.org. The *EvangeCube* is easy to use and to teach to children, and it is amazingly effective in countries around the world.

The *EvangeCube* displays various gospel pictures, including sinful humanity separated from a holy God, Jesus dying on the cross, Jesus buried in the tomb, Jesus risen from the dead, the cross as the only way to God, the choice between heaven and hell, and five ways to grow as a Christian. This ministry has prepared excellent teacher-training guides, including a short DVD and workbooks that explain how to use this tool effectively and how to train others to use it (including other adults, youth, children, and national believers). The *EvangeCube* comes in various sizes, from a tiny plastic cube that can hook to a child's backpack, to medium-sized cubes, to a "BIG CUBE" for classroom demonstration.

In just a short time, news of the *EvangeCube*—and through this tool the powerful message of the gospel of Jesus Christ—is spreading around the world. Teachers, missionaries, churches, and children are using this little cube to share God's plan of salvation effectively. Your mission-minded child will be excited about it!

Teaching Your Family to Use the *EvangeCube*

- What you need: One "BIG CUBE," *EvangeCube* teacher's workbook, the *EvangeCube* demonstration DVD, and a small *EvangeCube* for each person.

- What to do: Demonstrate the *EvangeCube*, watch the DVD, and have family members practice presenting different sections.

- Have one person use the "BIG CUBE" to share the gospel. Have your children follow along at the same time with their small cubes.

— 👥 FROM MY CHILDREN'S PERSPECTIVE —

IT'S COOL TO USE THE CUBE!
By Daniel Dunagan, age fifteen

What's neat about the *EvangeCube* is that it really grabs people's attention! Its pictures show how we all need God, how Jesus died on the cross for us, and how Jesus is the only "bridge" between people and God. I've used the *EvangeCube* on mission trips to Uganda, while helping in kids' church here at home, and with people in international airports.

The cube is really cool and interesting, and people are usually curious to talk about it. As I turn the cube to show different pictures, it also helps me to remember all the major points of sharing the gospel. It's quick and easy to use, and it really helps people to see how great God is!

◉ TEACHING OPPORTUNITY

Learn to Use Drama in Ministry

A simple dramatic presentation can be an effective way to share the gospel.

- *Mime:* Dress in black clothes, wear white gloves, and cover your face with white makeup. Without using words, act out simple messages.

- *Skits:* Use costumes, or props to teach basic stories, such as getting rid of sin.

- *Clowns:* Dress in clown costumes and give out candy or balloons to draw a crowd.

- *Human Video:* Act out or create motions for a song with a powerful message.

Leading Your Family in Doing a Live "Human Video"

- What you need: CD player, a song with a powerful message (such as "Asleep in the Light" by Keith Green or "The Champion" by Carman), appropriate costumes and props.

- What to do: Pray together for the Holy Spirit to anoint your family as you prepare and present your drama. Talk about using drama to explain a message. Have family members practice dramatizing different emotions, such as happiness, fear, excitement, confusion, etc. Listen to a song, and create motions to explain the meaning. Practice repeatedly.

- Share the song with the dramatic motions.

A Teen Mania Drama Testimony

Just yesterday I spoke with a fifteen-year-old from our church youth group, Caleb, who just returned from a Teen Mania mission outreach to New Zealand. When I asked him what stood out as a favorite highlight, Caleb shared about a time his team presented a drama about suicide. During their performance, a teenage girl ran out of the room, crying. When the girl returned, she shared how she was seriously contemplating suicide, but she realized God loved her and had a purpose for her life; and she prayed with the group to become a Christian!

TEACHING OPPORTUNITY

Learn How to Use Puppets

Puppets can be a great tool to help reach the lost. Learning puppetry skills can be fun, and knowing them provides a way for a child to participate actively in ministry outreaches.

Puppet Ministry for Beginners

*   *Step 1—Master mouth movements*
    Learn to synchronize the puppet's mouth with your voice
    (or the puppet's "voice" on a song or puppet recording). The
    puppet's mouth should open with every syllable, instead of
    merely opening and closing in a random snapping motion. The
    mouth should open wider on accented syllables, while opening
    only slightly on unaccented syllables. When moving the
    puppet's mouth, move only the puppet's bottom jaw (operated
    by your thumb). The top of the puppet's head (operated by
    your other four fingers) should remain still.

- *Step 2—Keep puppet's eye contact*
  Keep your puppet's head down so the audience can see its eyes. Don't have your puppet speak up to the ceiling or down to the floor. Keep the puppet's head looking around naturally without continually bobbing up and down.

- *Step 3—Show the entire puppet, but not the puppeteer!*
  Make sure the puppet's entire body can be seen, not just its head. If the puppet has arms, keep them in the front of the stage. If you are a puppeteer, don't let the audience see you, particularly your arm. And don't let anyone see an empty puppet not in use.

Training Your Family in Basic Puppet Ministry

- What you need: Puppets, a puppet stage, a CD player and a DVD player, a microphone, puppetry DVD (*Basic Techniques Puppetry Training* DVD by Puppet Productions is excellent for teaching beginning puppet skills), and a music tape or CD (easy puppet songs are "The Laughing Song" from Puppet Productions and "He's Got the Whole World in His Hands" from *Wee Sing Bible Songs*).

- What to do: Pray for God to help your family use puppets to share about Jesus effectively and to convey God's love for children. Distribute the puppets to your family and review the three steps above. Watch the *Basic Techniques Puppetry Training* DVD and follow the directions. Practice simple puppet songs: first *without* the puppet stage, then *with* the puppet stage.

- Present your puppet shows.

Let Your Light Shine!
A Mission-Minded Puppet Skit

Two puppets needed: "Ralph" (with a small flashlight) and "Bernie"

RALPH: (Enters with the flashlight, singing "This Little Light of Mine." As he gets to the verse "Hide it under a bushel—No!" Ralph is singing very loudly and waving the flashlight around. This can be done by attaching a small flashlight to a puppet's hand with wire or tape, and the puppet's arm can be moved by using a metal hanger attached to the puppet's arm or an official puppetry rod. Another option is to use a human-arm puppet that takes two arms to operate, one for the puppet's head and the other for the puppet's arm. This second method is my favorite because the puppet can hold a full-size flashlight for the skit.)

BERNIE: Excuuuse me . . . Uh . . . Yoo-hoo! What do you think you're doing?

RALPH: Who, me?

BERNIE: Yes, *you*, Ralph. What are you doing?

RALPH: Can't you see, Bernie? I'm letting my little light shine! I learned this cool song at church, and now I'm shining my light all over. See my neat flashlight? It really works gooooood.

BERNIE: Ralph! That's not what the song is talking about.

RALPH: What do you mean? It's not?

BERNIE: Of course not! "Letting your light shine" means that we're not afraid to tell other people about Jesus.

RALPH: Are you serious?

BERNIE: Yes, I'm serious. Jesus said that He is the Light of the World, but He also told us to be "lights" for Him by telling other people about His love.

RALPH: Wow! You mean I don't even need this flashlight?

BERNIE: No, silly! You just need boldness to share about Jesus. You could use your Bible or a story, but the important thing is that you do what God says and be a witness for Him.

RALPH: That sounds easy enough!

BERNIE: With Jesus, it *is* easy. And one more thing, Ralph . . .

RALPH: Yeah?

BERNIE: Do you see how bright it is up here? You hardly need a flashlight here because there's already so much light. But if you look down there (Have both puppets look behind the puppet stage) . . . it's dark!

RALPH: (Shining his flashlight down below the puppet stage) Wow! Look how good this flashlight shows up down there!

BERNIE: You see, Ralph, we need to spread the gospel of Jesus here at home, but did you know there are many places where people have never heard about Jesus? There are millions and *millions* of unreached people around the world, and someone's gotta *go* to them!

RALPH: Isn't that called being a "missionary"?

BERNIE: That's right, and we can *all* be missionaries. When we help fulfill the mission of Jesus, we're really letting our light shine!

RALPH: That sounds exciting, Bernie!

BERNIE: It really is; and every one of us needs to find God's purpose and plan for our lives and do our part in sharing His light around the world. Do you get it?

RALPH: You bet! I'm going to let my light shine for Jesus—especially to those who haven't heard about Him.

BERNIE: Good job, Ralph!

RALPH: (Singing as he begins to walk "downstairs" behind
          the puppet stage) "Ohhh, this little light of mine, I'm
          a'gonna let it shine. . . . Ohhhh NOOOOO!" (Make
          sound effects of Ralph falling down the stairs)

BERNIE: Ralph! Ralph! Are you all right?

RALPH: (Responding weakly) Yeah, but I really should have
          used the flashlight.

Q. How can we use puppets when we can't speak the language?

- Learn a few key words and phrases, translated into the foreign language, that the puppet can say (such as *hello, goodbye, yes, no, Hallelujah, Praise the Lord,* and *Jesus loves you*).

- Have the puppet simply make animal sounds. You can "interpret" what the puppet is saying; then an interpreter can translate for the people.

- Have the interpreter interpret what the puppet is saying.

- Teach your interpreter to use a puppet so you can have an interpreter puppet. Children (and adults) usually think this is funny.

- Teach a local worker to use puppets, and let him or her speak for the puppet in the local language. (When you leave the area, you could even give this worker a puppet or two to continue reaching children for Jesus.)

- Purchase an upbeat, contemporary Christian CD in the foreign language, and have the puppet mouth the words. Make sure that the words are appropriate, and practice synchronizing the movements.

- Purchase a prerecorded puppet skit in the foreign language, and practice having the puppets mouth the words. (Puppet

Productions has many prerecorded puppet skits available in Spanish.)

- Use a ventriloquist-style puppet, making animal sounds or saying "Hello" while walking up and down a street, as a drawing card. Have a local person walk with you as you invite children to come to a nearby meeting.

- Just have fun; have the puppets sing in English . . . and draw a curious crowd!

TEACHING OPPORTUNITY

Focus on Music and Worship Ministry

If your family is musical, take time to prepare songs for ministry. You may want to purchase some musical accompaniment CDs or practice with your own instruments. If possible, learn a song or a simple chorus in the language of the people you desire to reach, or be prepared to learn a song from a long-term missionary or national. Perhaps you could add some basic choreography or motions to help make your presentation more effective.

Even if you sing in English, or present an instrumental piece with no lyrics, music can be a powerful tool to draw people to hear the gospel. As you practice, prepare your heart to "minister"—not merely to "perform." Pray for God's Holy Spirit to soften hearts and to impact the people to whom you will minister.

Training Your Family in Music and Worship Ministry

- What you need: CD player, sound system, and one or two accompaniment tapes or CDs with a mission theme. Possible ideas: "Carry the Light" by Twila Paris or "Heart to Change the World" from Psalty's *Kids' Praise! 6: Heart to Change the World* CD. Have the words of the songs written out and available for practice.

- What to do: Pray together and discuss the importance of ministry, as opposed to mere musical "performance." Sing scales. Listen to the CD. Practice the songs. You will also want to practice with microphones and decide where everyone will stand. If desired, add hand motions or choreography.

- Sing the songs with a heart of worship.

Mission-Minded Music Lessons

If a member of your family enjoys music or has natural musical ability, it is good to encourage the development of this talent. Quality music lessons, faithful practice, and active participation in church worship are important. Even though it takes years of time, energy, and expense to establish musical excellence, this is an investment in future ministry. Developing musical talent in a godly child is like preparing a powerful spiritual weapon to win battles for the kingdom of God.

Realize Fitness Affects Your Family's Mission-Minded Purpose

A mission-minded family is healthy, active, and adventurous.

- *We are stewards of our bodies!* It's true that our focus needs to be on God's kingdom and His eternal purposes. Yet we also need to remember that our bodies are temples of God's Holy Spirit (1 Corinthians 6:19). We have been entrusted as stewards of these temples (our bodies); and, as parents, we must train our children to be good stewards of their bodies.

- *We exercise!* "Bodily exercise profits a little, but godliness is profitable for all things, having promise of the life that now is and of that which is to come" (1 Timothy 4:8). To put this into perspective, however, remember that Jesus and His disciples often walked several miles a day. I encourage mission-minded families to participate in athletics and physical activities, since God's mission-minded representatives need to be strong, healthy, and disciplined.

Reaching Out through Sports

Being involved in sports and athletic activities can help individual family members learn about teamwork, cooperation, friendship, evangelism, and community involvement—along with developing athletic skills and staying in shape, of course. If a child is athletic or enjoys participating in sports, encourage him or her to be a mission-minded child and develop these gifts for God's purposes. (At the same time, guard against sports commitments taking control of your family. Spiritual training and church participation should always be a higher priority.)

- If your child is on a sports team, encourage him or her to be a good example of godly sportsmanship and a Christian witness to fellow teammates and their families.

- Realize that athletic activities and games can be excellent drawing cards for Christian outreach and evangelism—both at home and overseas.

- A mission-minded athlete could travel to another country, arrange spontaneous athletic events, draw a crowd, and then share the Good News of Jesus!

A BUDDHIST COMES TO JESUS . . .
DURING CROSS-COUNTRY SEASON
About Patrick, at age fourteen

During high school, our oldest son, Patrick, had the opportunity to compete on a local cross-country team. During the season he became friends with a foreign exchange student from Thailand, Tip, who had been raised in a Buddhist family. After several lengthy conversations, Tip prayed to receive Jesus as his Lord and Savior. Though he later moved to another state and enrolled in college, Tip has continued to grow as a Christian. He celebrated his first "Christian" Christmas with our family, and he was baptized on Easter weekend in our family's pond. Tip is active in leadership at a strong Christian church: he works in the media department, leads a weekly "Royal Rangers" discipleship group for boys, and often shares his faith on his university campus.

I'm a Mission-Minded Soccer Mom

I've been a soccer mom, track mom, cross-country mom, and tennis mom. I've definitely "put in my time" going back and forth to games, meets, and matches. I've sat in the rain and stood in the snow, and I've encouraged my husband as he's coached. But most importantly, our family has had many opportunities to share about Jesus on the sidelines.

As a Christian mother, I love to keep focused on God's plans for my kids; but I don't regret the time we've invested in athletics. His purposes may require a healthy body, a daring mindset, and an adventurous attitude. Participating in sports is not just for competition and family entertainment; it can help our kids become disciplined, goal oriented, and even a witness for Jesus. On the sidelines, our family has met new friends and shared our faith—and we've had fun in the process. We keep balanced, and spiritual activities and church involvement are our priorities.

Even as a soccer mom, I cheer on my kids . . . toward God's goals!

Use Your Family's Skills . . . for Missions!

Instead of dwelling on what you lack or what you are unable to do, seek God for ways to use your abilities for His glory. Sometimes we consider only traditional missionary occupations, such as church work, medicine, Bible translation, or aviation; but the many needs overseas are as diverse as the talents you have been given.

- *Do you have construction experience?*
  You can help build a church or an orphanage. If you know how to paint, you could paint a Bible school or teach efficient painting techniques.

- *Do you have educational experience?*
  You can teach in an elementary school, hold a workshop to encourage local teachers, or introduce a curriculum to missionary families.

- *Do you have computer skills?*
  You can teach a missionary how to use a new software program, or you can conduct a training seminar overseas.

- *Do you know how to operate a VCR, a DVD player, or a film projector?*
  You can show the *JESUS* film, currently available in nearly one thousand languages, or another gospel film.

- *Do you speak English and have a college degree?*
  You can teach English as a second language. Many countries that are "closed" to missionaries are "open" to qualified teachers.

- *Do you have a happy family?*
  You can teach a marriage or parenting class or organize a seminar on being a godly father or mother.

- *Do you know how to wash your hands?*
  You can share information about cleanliness and sanitation in a remote village.

- *Do you know how to pray?*
  You can visit a country to pray and intercede or to teach a seminar on prayer.

Ideas for Helping the Poor

- Give clothes to needy children!

- Distribute toys or school supplies to an orphanage!

- Deliver gift boxes . . . or soap . . . or sheets . . . or food!

- Assist in a free health, dental, or midwifery clinic!

- Help distribute free Bibles or gospel tracts!

WHEN YOU DON'T FEEL "STIRRED" FOR SOULS

A Family VBS Story

One time when I wasn't feeling "in the mood" for missions, God renewed my passion for souls and challenged me afresh about the urgency of reaching the lost.

Jon and I were watching our little ones swim in our pond (which is more like a giant mud hole) and were talking with our fourteen-year-old son, Joshua, about an upcoming vacation Bible school closing service. Josh had been asked to preach alongside me, so he was trying to decide whether or not to say yes. And if he agreed to do it, he was trying to figure out what he could share.

Right at that moment our four-year-old daughter, Caela, stepped out too deep—and, without making a sound, she began to sink. Jon yelled, "Josh, get Caela!" Immediately—clothes, shoes, and all—Joshua leaped into the water, swam over to little Caela, and quickly pulled her out. Once we saw she was fine, Jon turned to Josh and said, "There is your sermon!"

All day long, I too had been thinking and praying about my message. Specifically, I was trying to decide how to minister to both the children and the adults who would be present, including some visiting parents who had likely never been in church before. It was going to be the final night of a weeklong VBS, and I was scheduled to share a "stirring" message about the importance of "getting out there and winning the lost." At the moment, however, I wasn't feeling very "stirred" myself.

Of course, I have a heart for missions and evangelism. It's what we do. It's our life. But quite honestly, at the moment I was more concerned with how to delicately preach a "strong" missions message—without offending those unchurched parents.

The next day, when Joshua and I arrived at the church early for preservice prayer, we were surprised to see many of the VBS workers crying. Their news was sobering and shocking. Just the night before, four children who attended VBS tragically lost their dad. The young father had been suddenly killed in a work accident.

This was one of those unchurched families I'd been thinking about. Only two days earlier, one of these boys received Jesus. Only one day earlier, after learning how children can be mighty in prayer, this same little boy filled out a prayer card that read, "Please pray for my Mommy and Daddy to know Jesus."

Who could have known how serious that little prayer would be?

Who could have known that in less than twenty-four hours that daddy's life would be over and that he would be face to face with eternity . . . either in heaven or in hell?

Who could have known?

As we prayed for the family, tears streamed down my cheeks. I was challenged afresh about the urgency of the gospel. How could I not be stirred about reaching the lost? How could I have been more concerned about offending unsaved parents than caring for their souls?

That night, Joshua and I both preached to a church full of children and adults about the importance of reaching the lost—even when we don't feel like it. Just like Joshua simply jumped in to rescue Caela, we need to rescue the lost. When our heavenly Father says, "Go!" we need to instantly obey! Joshua told the audience, "When Dad shouted at me to get my little sister, I didn't have to pray about it to see if it was God's will or not. I just had to jump in and get her!"

Over the years, specific life-and-death situations (at home and overseas) have challenged us to renew our passion for missions and the lost. Right at this moment, whether or not we realize it or can see them, multitudes of precious people are dying without Jesus Christ. Our Father sees them. If God calls us to reach out and help with a rescue, may we be ones who instantly leap to obey!

CHAPTER 9

You *Can* Go!

Taking a Mission Trip with Your Family

For many families, taking an overseas mission trip with a child (or perhaps several children) sounds utterly impossible. "How could our family afford it?" "How could we ever take that much time off work?" "How is it possible to travel with kids?" "But what about school?"

These are all legitimate questions, but more importantly, why not ask, *Dear Lord, would You ever want our family (or me, or one of my children, or a group from our school, or a team from our church) to go on a mission outreach?*

If God answers, "Yes," then the only legitimate questions to ask are *When?* and *Where?* and, in faith, *Well, Lord, then how do You want us to obey?*

Instead of responding with fear and doubt like Zacharias (Luke 1:18), have a willing heart like Mary (Luke 1:38), when she said, "Let it be to me according to your word." If God calls you or your child to missionary work, He will open the way for you, and He will provide more than enough of His grace and provision.

Q. But what if I'm at the peak of my career?

On the day Jesus called Peter to be a "fisher of men," Peter's nets were bursting with fish (Luke 5:6–7). Most likely it was the best day of Peter's fishing career, but Jesus called him to drop everything and follow Him (Matthew 4:18–20)! Jesus also called a rich young ruler, but this man was unwilling to surrender his money and his security (Matthew 19:16–22). If Jesus asks *you* to follow Him to the mission field, which of these two responses will *your* answer most closely resemble?

Q. But what if I just got married?

Congratulations! As you begin your life together, this is a great time to readjust your priorities and seek God's will for you as a married couple. Many newlyweds have gone straight from their wedding to the mission field. Read about young missionaries such as Adoniram and Nancy Judson or Jim and Elisabeth Elliot. Another perspective, from the Old Testament, presents a principle of newly married men being exempt from war and encouraged to stay home for a year to establish their marriage foundation (Deuteronomy 24:5). Early married life is a perfect time to find a godly mission-minded balance, with a fervent commitment to marriage and a lifelong commitment to God's purposes.

Q. But what if I still have children at home?

My husband always laughs when he hears this excuse. "Oh, that's right," he says. "You could *never* travel with kids!" But then he grins and raises his eyebrows, because we never traveled *before* we had children! For us, raising and training our children are a primary calling; yet through *every* season of our parenthood (pregnancy, chasing toddlers and little ones, homeschooling, raising teenagers and keeping up with their activities, and sending young adults to college), God is continually calling us to be an active part of world evangelization.

Sometimes our entire family goes on mission outreaches together. Other times Jon goes by himself or takes one of our older children. We've gone together as a couple or as a couple with a nursing baby and a few other children. (We've been blessed to have the option of godly parents, relatives, and friends who have taken turns caring for our children while we minister overseas on short-term trips.) Each time God calls us to a specific outreach, we pray and seek His will for that particular mission trip . . . and then we obey!

Q. But what if I'm in the prime of my life?

Does God deserve less? Midlife is a great time to readjust your priorities in order to reach the world! Try a short-term outreach (either you, or your spouse, or together as a couple, or together with your children) to minister and to seek God's will. Another option is to attend a short-term mission training school as a family, such as YWAM's six-month Crossroads Discipleship Training School.

There's No Excuse!

Our good friends Nels and Lorrie had every reason to stay home when God called their family to full-time missionary work. They had seven children still living at home, including little children and a son just graduating from high school, along with an elderly mother who lived with them. Lorrie was having health problems due to several miscarriages. And they had no financial support!

Even so, both Nels and Lorrie felt in their hearts God calling their family to start a Bible school on a remote island in the Philippines. So what did they do? They went—with all seven children and Nels' eighty-seven-year-old mother! And to top it off, they invited a paraplegic friend to join them! They must have been quite a sight as they arrived on that remote Filipino island of Catanduanes: seven exhausted children, luggage everywhere, Grandma with her walker, and Jeff in his wheelchair!

But God was so faithful. The family adjusted better than expected, God provided for every need, the Filipino people loved and appreciated their family's example, and the tropical sunshine helped improve Lorrie's health. Today their Bible school is established and growing strong, with graduates pioneering many Christian churches in unreached areas and on other remote islands.

Even with every excuse to stay home, Nels and Lorrie went!

From Texas to China

Another wonderful couple, Tom and Liz, along with their four young children, moved from their large home in Texas to a very small apartment in China. They began teaching English as a second language and started reaching out to young Chinese college students in the few crowded rooms they now called home. That was only the beginning! Since that time this mission-minded family has lived in many places throughout the world, including Costa Rica, India, and Malaysia. Tom and Liz now have eight mission-minded children (some of whom are adults), and their entire family is reaching people around the globe!

GO YE INTO ALL THE WORLD

A missions hymn, by James McGranahan (1840–1907)

Far, far away, in heathen darkness dwelling,
Millions of souls forever may be lost;
Who, who will go, salvation's story telling,
Looking to Jesus, minding not the cost?

"All pow'r is given unto Me,
All pow'r is given unto Me,
Go ye into all the world and preach the gospel,
And lo, I am with you always."

See o'er the world wide open doors inviting,
Soldiers of Christ, arise and enter in!
Christians, awake! your forces all uniting,
Send forth the gospel, break the chains of sin.

"Why will ye die?" the voice of God is calling,
"Why will ye die?" re-echo in His name;
Jesus hath died to save from death appalling,
Life and salvation, therefore go proclaim.

God speed the day, when those of ev'ry nation
"Glory to God!" triumphantly shall sing;
Ransomed, redeemed, rejoicing in salvation,
Shout Hallelujah, for the Lord is King.

Q. But what if my child wants to go on a mission trip and I'm afraid he or she is too young?

You may want to consider accompanying your child on a short-term children's mission outreach, such as YWAM's King's Kids or a Teen Mania outreach for preteens. Take seriously God's calling for you as a parent or teacher to nurture your child's desire and to adequately train and equip your child for this possibility. Let's encourage our children to pray regularly for world needs and to learn all they can about world missions.

Q. But what if my child needs to focus on school right now?

If you have a high school or college student interested in missions, encourage him or her to check out short-term opportunities with mission organizations such as Teen Mania, YWAM, Teen Missions, Master's Commission or through your own church or denomination.

Along with encouraging youth in what they do *for* God, especially encourage their personal walk *with* God. Challenge them to develop their relationship with God and to guard their relationships with others, keeping their lives pure and set apart for God's calling and purpose. One of the biggest hindrances to a young person fulfilling his or her calling to missions is marrying someone—even someone who is nice and loves the Lord—who is not also called to world missions. Communicate to your child that if God has given a desire and a calling for missions *at* a young age, He wants him or her to prepare for this calling *from* a young age! There is a time to focus on educational preparation, but encourage your child to "seek first the kingdom of God" (Matthew 6:33).

Q. But what if we have a large family?

What a blessing! So did many missionary heroes, including the founders of the Salvation Army, William and Catherine Booth, who had eight children, and African missionary John G. Lake, who had a dozen children (seven with his first wife and then, after she died, five with his second wife). Some missionary organizations may limit the number of children they allow, or "prefer," their missionaries to have, but there are always other options available. Your big family can be a great benefit to many missionary ministries.

Large families are common in many developing countries. If you have substantial parenting experience, others will highly regard your opinions. Your children and teenagers can be involved in your ministry, especially if you have trained them to be mission-minded. Buying airline tickets for many family members obviously will cost more; but to God, that makes no difference! Your monthly living expenses in a foreign country may be even less than they were previously.

Schooling is a major challenge and expense for many missionary families. For large homeschooling families, however, the children's education can continue nearly the same as before. If God is calling your family to missions, He will direct you and provide all your needs.

Here are a few other ideas. Perhaps Mom and Dad can go together on a mission trip (and perhaps enjoy a second honeymoon before or after the mission outreach) while the kids enjoy a few weeks at Grandma's. Or you can all work together (praying, seeking God, and raising support) to send one parent or teenager on a short-term outreach. You can even establish a new family tradition: when each child reaches a certain age (e.g., sixteen or eighteen), you will present that teenager with an airline ticket for a summer mission trip.

If your quiver is full of arrows (see Psalm 127:3–5), don't limit God's ability to send them wherever He wants them to go!

Q. But what if I'm getting too old? Isn't it too late for my family to make a change?

Consider Moses, Abraham, Sarah, and other mighty men and women of God who began their ministries later in life. It's never too late to obey God's call!

I once read about a woman in her mid-eighties who travels throughout the world, sharing the gospel. As I stared at her photograph, I marveled at her adventurous attitude. She reminded me of eighty-five-year-old Caleb, ready at last to take his inheritance in the Promised Land, shouting, "Give me this mountain!" (see Joshua 14:6–12). In the photo, this elderly woman—with a huge smile on her face—was sitting on the back of a mule in a remote mountainous area. Her white hair wasn't a hindrance but an asset to her ministry. Because of her age, nationals honored and respected her; and because of her willingness, many have come to Christ.

Young in Faith

Bob and Carol were nearing retirement, but they longed for something more in their lives. One day, during a time of discouragement and seeking direction, they came to our home for dinner. Jon and I shared some exciting mission testimonies and challenged Bob and Carol to do something different. We invited them to teach at a village pastors' conference overseas. Despite major challenges, this elderly couple decided to *go*—and their lives have never been the same.

Overseas, they were challenged by the need for godly discipleship and pastoral training. But instead of just complaining about the need, these two were led by God to do something about it. After much prayer, they made the big decision to move overseas as full-time missionaries.

This last year (at Thanksgiving), we met again for dinner; but this time we were near their home in Kampala, Uganda. As we shared our strange holiday food (including zebra and ostrich), this couple shared highlights from the past few years. Over ten Bible schools are training ministers all over East Africa. Over 1,500 pastors have graduated from their yearlong program. Mobile health clinics and volunteer doctors are ministering to the physical needs of the people. Carol teaches women cooking and sewing skills, enabling them to earn extra income. As Bob and Carol shared their vision for an orphanage they were about to open, my mind went back to that day in our living room only a few years earlier. This incredible couple wondered if God's ministry for them was over . . . but it had barely begun!

Q. But what if I don't have anything to offer?

So you don't think you have special talents. You can't speak a foreign language. You don't even like to go camping. Well, you are in good company!

- **Gladys Aylward** initially was turned away in her attempt to become a missionary. Yet eventually, in 1932, she went to China and became a beloved Christian servant. In her own words, Aylward thanked God that "one so insignificant, uneducated, and ordinary in every way could be used to His glory for the blessing of His people in poor, persecuted China" (from the back cover of *Gladys Aylward: Missionary to China*, Heroes of the Faith Series, by Sam Wellman, Barbour Publishing, 1998). (For more about Aylward's exciting missionary life, watch the classic movie *The Inn of the Sixth Happiness*, starring Ingrid Bergman. Although not completely accurate, this wholesome film is mission-minded and inspirational.)

- **Bruce Olson** was shy and weak as a child, hating outdoor activities and Scouting. Yet God chose him to reach the remote and primitive Motilone people of Colombia. Much of this tribe has now turned to Christianity, and the Motilones are reaching surrounding areas with the gospel of Jesus Christ! (Read Bruce's book, *Bruchko*, for the exciting details.)

- **Elisabeth Elliot** wondered why God had chosen her. She couldn't sing, and she wasn't a nurse or a gifted linguist; but God has used this woman mightily through her missionary work and inspirational writing! (Read her story in *Through Gates of Splendor* and *The Savage, My Kinsman*.)

There is no perfect time to step into missionary work. At every stage in life there will always be challenges to overcome and barriers to cross. No matter what your current situation, God can make a way for you. He does not expect you to use what you *don't* have; He simply expects you to love and serve Him with what you *do* have. As you obey the Lord, step by step, He will multiply your gifts and talents for His purposes. It is not all about doing things *for* God, but being *with* God: living in His presence, hearing His voice and direction, and being available to serve Him—through His strength and gifts, not your own.

🌐 TEACHING OPPORTUNITY

Practical Steps for "Stepping Out"

If God has given you or your child a specific direction for the future, realize that He spoke this now because He wants you to *do something now*. If He didn't want you to do anything right away, why would He bother to tell you at this early time? If God has given you His direction, it's likely He wants you to begin—by preparing your heart, learning, or praying—to pave the way for future outreach.

Gather Information

- Begin preparing by praying and interceding for the specific people you desire to reach. At the same time, learn everything you can about them. If you have a burden for a particular country, do some research at the library or on the Internet, or write to the country's international embassy for information.

- Find out what you would need for travel: passport, visa, inoculations?

- If you are interested in a particular missionary organization, write or call for information. Compare and evaluate the opportunities they have available; and explore their focus, policies, and particular mission. How long are their mission outreaches? Are there educational requirements? Do they train team members? How extensive is their training? What are their views on children and families? Can children be involved in the ministry outreach? What are their opinions on schooling? What are their basic theological beliefs? What is the living environment like? What is their leadership or authority structure? Is there potential for career missionary opportunities? And, of course, how much will it cost (and is there training for raising support)?

Seek Godly Counsel

- As you gather information, pray for direction and seek godly counsel from other mature believers, from missionaries you know, from your pastor or youth leader (if you're a young person) . . . and listen to their advice!

Research Airline and Travel Prices

- If you are considering traveling on your own or taking care of your own travel arrangements, check with a local travel agency for approximate travel costs.

- You can usually get a better price if you check with several travel agencies or directly with international airline companies.

- Some travel organizations have missionary discounts. We have found over the years, however, that missionary travel restrictions and date limitations are usually too difficult to work with. We can generally beat the price by shopping around or looking into different international connections.

- Compare various travel award programs. For years, we traveled on whatever airline had the lowest fare, regardless of routes or services. After years of accumulating a hodgepodge of expiring mileage on various airlines, we decided on one airline to use on a regular basis. By using its mileage award program, we now earn at least one free international trip each year.

Get Your Passport

- If you or your child are considering going on a mission trip someday and haven't yet applied for a passport, what are you waiting for? This is one thing you can do right away. If you are serious about being available for God, get ready! You can pick up a passport application at your local post office, get a passport photo, show identification, and then submit the application and required fee.

- When traveling, it is vital to keep your passport either with you at all times or in a secure location. This is your most important travel document. Without your passport, you cannot legally remain in a foreign country, travel to another foreign country, or return home. Your passport guarantees your citizenship and is your best form of identification.

Find Out If You Need Travel Visas

- Certain countries require a visa, in addition to a passport, for entrance. A visa is a stamp or sticker inside your passport granting permission to enter a particular country for a designated time. Contact a travel agency or check the Internet for international embassy addresses to inquire about specific requirements for the country you wish to enter. Travel agencies often pay for necessary visa or passport photos if you purchase your tickets through them.

Find Out If You Need Inoculations

- Pick up international travel inoculation certificates from a doctor. In many developing countries, certain health requirements are necessary for entrance.

- Some inoculations require a series of shots taken over time. Other recommended inoculations may be unnecessary. Opinions differ on the potential risks of certain inoculations, so seek advice and seek the Lord.

Short-Term Mission Travel Tips

Q. Do you have any packing tips?

* *Pack light.* When selecting clothes for a short-term mission trip, be sure to pack lightly. Clothing is often washed daily in other countries, so only a few changes are usually necessary. In warmer climates, lightweight, quick-drying clothing is best. Select clothes that coordinate with a few basic colors and that will be appropriate for the work planned. As you leave home, check for the three most important items: passport, tickets, and money. (All the rest is luxury!)

* *Pack modest clothes.* Be sensitive to the culture of the people to whom you will minister. Clothing that is perfectly modest at home may be perceived as immoral in another culture. In many places, women cannot wear pants, and neither women nor men can wear shorts. In some areas, women's necks and ankles must be covered. In other locales, certain colors (such as red) are considered taboo.

    Modesty is a heart issue; but at times it can be "relative," depending on cultural practices. Many times as I've traveled through African or Asian jungles in my khaki safari skirt, I've secretly wished for pants. Pants would be more practical and modest when I'm standing in the back of a truck with my skirt blowing in the wind or as I climb over things. It's funny to see women in these same places remove their shirts to nurse their babies while sitting in the front row of a church or use a pit toilet or shower with no door. In their culture, these very "immodest" actions—by our standards—are perfectly acceptable.

- *Pack with sensitivity.* As Christians, we must be culturally sensitive and as inoffensive as possible when selecting items to bring. (For example, check the wallet photos you take with you for culturally inappropriate dress. A family photo at the beach could be devastating to your ministry!)

  You may want to bring small gifts and thank you cards for people who show you kindness or for people with whom you stay.

A Few Extra Hints

- When packing, try to bring no more than one suitcase per person, in addition to your carryon luggage. On short-term mission trips, the second allotted suitcase is usually used for ministry supplies or gifts for missionaries and national ministers. When our family travels, I often limit my personal luggage to my carryon bag.

- As my husband constantly tells me, don't cram your suitcases too full. If you have to force your luggage to close, remove a few items (which is much easier said than done!) to prevent broken hinges or zippers.

- Fill your shoes with underwear and socks, and then stuff them inside a pair of socks to protect other clothing.

- Instead of folding your clothes, try rolling them. You will fit more clothes in your suitcase, you will see everything at once, and your clothes will get less wrinkled.

- I have found that a small spray bottle is excellent to have along for straightening messy hair, cleaning children's dirty hands and faces, and spraying wrinkled clothes when an iron is unavailable.

- Take along a small empty duffle bag to use for day-long outreaches or to accommodate for a lack of space later.

- Because of varying electrical systems around the world, you may want to research on the Internet to find out if you need to bring a converter or adapter. Some countries (such as North American countries and parts of South and Central America, the Pacific, and the Caribbean) have an across-the-board standard of 110 volts, while others (such as European and African countries) have a standard voltage of 220. Without a proper converter, your electrical appliances (hairdryer, curling iron, cell phone, and camera battery charger, etc.) will be unusable.

A Few Notes about Travel Money

- When traveling to a Third World country, you usually need to bring cash. Many developing countries will not accept traveler's checks, while others will accept them, but at a low exchange rate. If you are departing from the United States, bring crisp one-hundred-dollar bills in order to get the best exchange rate for your money.

- When traveling as a foreigner in technologically advanced countries, credit cards are often required to secure a rental car or a hotel room. In developing countries, however, a credit card is of no use.

- A calculator is helpful for calculating confusing exchange rates and prices. Chances are your cell phone includes a calculator.

- Worldwide communication has dramatically improved in recent years, with expanding Internet and cell phone coverage, especially in international cities. A cell phone is still of no use in many areas, although we are often pleasantly surprised. Many developing countries skipped the step of establishing telephone landlines and went directly to building cell phone towers; and sometimes we receive better cell phone coverage in remote villages than we do at home! At other times a cell phone may not be able to make calls, but text messages will get through.

- To avoid being a victim of thieves, wear a money belt instead of using a purse or wallet. Also, to get better deals (and to avoid being cheated), try to have a faithful national friend assist you with shopping.

Q. What are some health tips for international travel?

- In addition to travel inoculations, be sure to secure any necessary medications you may need (such as an antimalarial drug).

- Carry at least a thirty-day supply of any necessary medication, along with a copy of your prescriptions.

- If you wear eyeglasses or contact lenses, take extra pairs and a copy of your eye prescription. (Because of dust and heavy pollution in some developing countries, many people find it difficult to wear contact lenses.)

- Be careful to drink clean water (professionally bottled or thoroughly boiled and purified). Some people travel with a small water purifier.

- When packing, always keep your medications, passport, tickets, and other important papers and valuables in your carryon luggage. Because there is always the possibility of luggage being misplaced, don't pack in your luggage any items you would desperately miss. Put all liquids and lotions in plastic bags, leaving room for expansion due to air pressure while flying and—because of security regulations—pack these items in your checked suitcase rather than your carryon luggage.

- Include in your carryon luggage a small first-aid kit and over-the-counter medications for upset stomach, diarrhea, motion sickness, and constipation.

- You may also want to bring sunscreen and a mosquito net in your checked luggage. You may opt to purchase these items overseas, but only if you will have time for shopping and access to them.

Q. Do you have any other practical advice?

- *Learn a few foreign phrases.* Introduce yourself and your children to basic phrases and simple worship songs in the language of the people you desire to reach. Buy a small dictionary or a teaching CD with commonly used words. Commit yourself to learn at least a friendly greeting and a word of thankfulness.

- *Take care of things at home.* There are many details to take care of before leaving home. Decide whether you are comfortable with just locking your home or if you need to arrange for a friend or relative to house-sit. Cancel or hold newspaper subscriptions, and have your mail held at the post office. Schedule someone to mow your lawn, shovel snow, care for animals or plants, etc.

- *Do your best to resolve relationship problems.* Before leaving on a mission trip, make sure you are on good terms with friends and extended family members. If there has been unforgiveness or hard feelings in the past, repent and ask forgiveness for any wrongs you have done, and do your best to make things right. Even though you will likely be busy with travel details, now is the time to get things worked out. Being separated by distance will probably only hamper your communication and any hope of future reconciliation. Unforgiveness could hinder your prayers and your ministry.

Some Things We Don't Want to Think About

- Secure any necessary details concerning your family's health insurance, life insurance, and wills.

- If traveling overseas, prayerfully determine ahead of time what you want to happen to your body in the event of your unlikely death. On my husband's first trip to Africa, an elderly pastor traveling with him came down with cerebral malaria and died within one day. This man would have preferred to be buried in Africa—a *much* less expensive option than transporting his body back to the United States—but he hadn't clearly conveyed that to his family before the trip. The result was confusion, added stress, and tremendous hassles with the foreign government.

- Whatever you do, don't be afraid! As Christians, we should already be "crucified with Christ" (Galatians 2:20). Your mission goal, of course, is not to go and be martyred for Christ! The goal is to go and come back . . . so you can share an inspiring mission report . . . and then go again!

We Died before We Came

When James Calvert went out as a missionary to the cannibals of the Fiji Islands, the ship captain tried to turn him back, saying, *"You will lose your life and the lives of those with you if you go among such savages."*

To that, Calvert replied, *"We died before we came here."*

An "Opportunity of a Lifetime"

A few days ago I received a sobering e-mail from a mission-minded college student. A friend of hers, a sixteen-year-old girl, had gone on a short-term mission outreach; and on the last day of the trip, while the team was having a fun free day, this girl accidentally drowned in the ocean.

I've had such a burden for this whole situation. The girl, one of ten children, was very sweet and had already been on several other mission trips. I've been praying for her parents, siblings, church, friends, and mission team. It's very hard and very sad.

In hindsight, I found the promotional ad for this mission trip a bit unsettling:

> Don't miss the opportunity of a lifetime! Pack your bags and hop on a plane . . . where you will set foot on one of the most beautiful tropical landscapes in the world! During your ministry days, you will reach out in schools, parks, villages and churches. . . . You will have the opportunity to minister through practical drama, testimonies, and service projects. On your free day, be ready make the most of the sandy beaches, catch some sun, hit the waves, and cool off in the ocean. The summer can't get any better than this!

Who would have known a precious teenage missionary would "hit the waves" . . . and never come back? I know the church that sponsored this outreach, and it's a fabulous mission-minded church with a great world vision. But what do they do now? They grieve. They support the girl's family and friends. They seek God's wisdom for future precautions so this won't happen again.

I heard about this situation as I was completing this chapter, and I felt I couldn't ignore it. As mission-minded families, we do need to realize that international travel can be dangerous. A mission trip is not just about fun times and exotic destinations. Travel today is easier (and safer) than ever; but we still need to seek God's direction. Yes, there is risk involved; but we still need to *go*.

As a final note, at this precious girl's funeral service, several people surrendered their lives to Jesus Christ. Her father addressed the congregation and encouraged other mission-minded families not to be moved by fear because of this situation. This man urged everyone in the audience to continue to support youth missions, and he even shared how he and his wife had prayerfully decided to send another daughter on the church's next mission outreach.

Taking Photographs

- Taking photographs during your mission trip will enhance your experience and help you remember this time for years to come.

- Before you go, know how to use your camera (especially if it is new), and make certain that everything is in good working order. Make sure you have everything you need (batteries, memory cards, or film, etc.).

- Thinking you may be "taking their soul," people in remote areas may be hesitant for you to take their photo. Or a local police officer may see you taking a photograph of an interesting bridge and accuse you of spying for the CIA. (Avoid wearing army camouflage for this same reason!) In other places, both adults and children may beg you to take their picture. Be sensitive to cultural differences.

- It is great to capture your special memories on film or video, for your own sake as well as to help share your mission vision when you return home. But may your first impression be a loving smile and a courteous greeting, not that of an impersonal tourist flashing pictures.

Traveling with Young Children

- When traveling with children, put together a small backpack for each child with activity books, art supplies, reading materials, small toys, and a few snacks.

- If you are traveling with a ministry team or with a large family, assign each person a partner to help keep track of everyone.

- When spending an extended time in an international airport, look for a nursery or a children's play area. Many major airports even provide cribs for little ones to sleep.

- In order to alleviate the effects of increased air pressure, attempt to nurse or bottle-feed your baby during takeoff and landing. Don't feed your baby for a while beforehand, so that he or she will be a little hungry when the plane is taking off. For young children, sucking on a piece of candy or chewing a piece of gum will help.

- While traveling, watch for people with whom you can share Jesus Christ. You and your child can meet people from all over the world in an international airport, many with nothing to do as they wait for their flight. Be prepared to witness by packing small New Testaments or gospel tracts in your carry-on luggage.

Food and Mission Trips

- Bring along snack foods, such as crackers, beef jerky, or a bag of trail mix.

- Expose your children to different kinds of food, and train them to eat whatever is set before them. This may be challenging at times. Our family has eaten nearly raw dog meat and fried intestines, sea slugs with oyster sauce, chicken feet, snake, eel, and monkey. Encourage your children to think of it as a great adventure.

- If your family has a usual eating preference (such as vegetarian, vegan, or particular food allergies), ask God for extra grace, and clearly explain any necessary requirements with those who need to know. Be willing—with a positive attitude—to be flexible. Adapt as much as possible to cultural norms.

- Realize that the most challenging things to eat will make the best stories back home!

Discipline of Children

- Be very cautious about the physical discipline of your children, especially if you are staying with people from another culture. In some countries, spanking is not practiced and is seen as abuse.

- Pray for extra grace and patience, and prepare your kids to be well behaved. Cultural misunderstandings are especially common on short-term outreaches.

Homeschooling and Missions

Homeschooling Overseas

Years ago, many mission organizations had negative attitudes toward homeschooling, believing it could hinder missionaries from their "primary" responsibility of ministry. (As parents, raising our children should be our primary ministry.) However, as homeschooling has become more mainstream, this option has become more encouraged.

Yes, teaching your children is very time consuming and demanding; but all homeschooling parents have to deal with that. What parent isn't busy, with time demanded on every front—home, ministry, church, and work? Homeschooling families know this route takes work and is often hard, but we make the sacrifice. Why? For some, it's simply the best of several (perhaps all of them challenging) options. For many, it's what the Lord has shown us to do. But regardless of your family's educational decision, it's important to remember that God has called parents to train their children; and the ultimate responsibility should not be relinquished to anyone else.

Missions work may, at times, involve periods of family separation. God may call you to travel short term into a volatile area, where it would be extremely dangerous to take your children. Sometimes one spouse may travel alone to a remote village, or perhaps a husband and wife may go together. But for the most part, God has called you to be a family. Homeschooling and missions fit together perfectly. You have the flexibility to travel, and your children can be involved in ministry. You *can* do it!

Homeschooling on a Short-term Mission Trip

- If taking a short-term mission trip, immerse yourself and your children in the culture you are reaching to make the most of your outreach.

- When our children travel overseas on short-term outreaches (for two or three weeks), they usually leave behind all of their regular schoolwork, other than their Bible and journal, in order to have time for all there is to learn and enjoy.

- Have your children compare their experiences to typical life back home. Taste the local food. Attempt to communicate in the local language. Watch unique characteristics of the people. Learn about the local geography, arts, and technology (or lack of it). Note different animals, birds, and plant life. Soak in the sights, smells, and sounds; and enjoy your time of ministry. Think of it as an extended field trip and an exciting cross-cultural experience.

Homeschooling on a Long-term Outreach

*   When living among another people group for an extended time, you and your children will need to develop a routine for regular school subjects.

*   Instead of isolating your children, encourage them to play with nationals and to learn their language. A child can often learn a foreign language by exposure alone.

*   Most likely you will not have access to resources found in a quality library. A solution to this challenge is to acquire a good supply of CD reference tools and educational DVDs. Get a laptop that can connect to a car battery, enabling your child to access important reference information anywhere in the world—even when Internet access is unavailable.

*   Begin to build your own library or work with other missionary families to build an educational library. Perhaps your church, mission partners, or a local school group from home could specifically support you in the area of your schooling. They can help you with challenges, send interesting Internet links or encouraging care packages, or simply be available (through e-mail or traditional mail) to assist your educational endeavors.

The Culture Shock of Coming Home

Individuals and families are often unprepared for the culture shock and emotional letdown following a mission outreach. It may be frustrating to find friends and church members unconcerned about your experience or uncaring about the world's needs. The blessings of home may suddenly appear wasteful and extravagant, and you may feel critical toward others or confused about what to do next.

In their article on Crosswalk.com, "Mission Trip Anyone?" David and Laurie Callihan share about the positive (yet challenging) impact of a mission trip: "For our daughter, returning home was heartbreaking. Rebekah cried off and on for a week straight. Her heart was changed as a result of this experience. She has wanted to be a nurse since she was a child. Now she is dreaming of possibly returning as a missionary nurse to this remote village, to share the gospel message of the love of Jesus with these underprivileged children. This experience was a supernatural intervention by the Holy Spirit in the life of a young Christian girl."

🌐 TEACHING OPPORTUNITY

Prepare to Share
(It's not over when it's over)

At the conclusion of an outreach, prepare to share with others about your experience. Ask yourself questions that will help you evaluate your time of ministry, including both positive aspects and negative challenges. Lead those in your family who went on the trip in discussing how you adjusted to change and in summarizing highlights of your journey.

Be prepared to share an encouraging testimony of your experiences. Have a one-minute version (for the casual inquirer), a three- to five-minute version with a few pictures (for an information update for a class, youth group, home group, or school), and a more detailed summary of about ten to fifteen minutes (for your church or more intent audiences). Include in this summary the overall picture of where you went, why you went, what you saw, and what you did, as well as a few specific examples and personal testimonies. Keep your reports brief, positive, and full of enthusiasm.

When you come back, your vision for missions should be contagious. Even a brief contact could spread God's heart for the world to others.

Post-Outreach Debriefing with Your Family

Our Expectations

- How did this trip compare with what I (we) expected?

- How has my (our) view of world missions changed?

- Is my (our) view of a "missionary" different from before?

- What did I (we) think of the people? The culture? The food? The transportation?

Our Positive Experiences

- What aspects of the culture did I (we) enjoy most?

- What person stands out most—in a positive way?

- Share a specific positive ministry experience.

- Think of one person in particular who was helped by my (our) ministry.

Our Greatest Frustrations

- Describe any frustrations you may have had with the culture.

- What was your greatest frustration in ministry? With the team?

- Was it challenging to adjust to the local people? The food? The transportation system? The living conditions? Time considerations?

- What could I (we) have done to make the trip more positive?

Our Personal/Family/Class Evaluation

- How well did I (we) portray Christ? Through my attitudes? Through our unity?

- Did I (we) cooperate well? with missionaries? With nationals?

- How did I (we) do during travel times?

- Did I (we) adequately prepare for this outreach?

- Do I (we) appreciate things that I (we) previously took for granted, such as hot water, toilets, sanitation, home?

Our Ideas for Future Improvement

- How could this trip have been more beneficial to me (us)?

- How could I (we) have prepared better to help those I was (we were) ministering to?

- What area and attitudes do I (we) need to work on most?

Our plan to share a positive report with others

- How can I (we) effectively and briefly share about this experience?

- If I (we) had only one minute to share, what would I (we) say?

- If I (we) had only three to five minutes to share, what would I (we) say?

- If I (we) had ten to fifteen minutes to share, what would I (we) say?

- How can this experience help encourage world missions?

Our new view for the future

Taking your first mission trip is only the beginning. Upon returning home, it's important to look to the future and seek God for your next step. Here are a few questions to consider during your debriefing time:

- What does God want me (us) to do when I (we) get home?

- How can I (we) continue to reach out to the people I (we) just visited?

- Does God want me (us) to pray more? Give more? Recruit others?

- How can I (we) reach out more to my (our) neighbors and community?

- What would I (we) think about the possibility of another outreach?

- Would I (we) be open to long-term missions?

- How can I (we) prepare for the future?

IN PURSUIT OF THE PERFECT FAMILY VACATION

By Laurel Diacogiannis

What is your dream of the Perfect Family Holiday? Relaxing on a Caribbean cruise? Tanning on the beaches of Hawaii? Or, perhaps, shopping in New York City?

What are your children's ideas of the Perfect Family Holiday? A week at Disney World? A houseboat trip on Lake Shasta? Or, maybe, snow skiing in Colorado?

Although all of the above sound like quite a treat to me, my children have humbled me, this year, by asking for a very different type of family holiday. I shouldn't be surprised, however, because I have encouraged them for many years to look more toward the needs of others than toward their own pursuit of pleasure.

For many years, I have had a heart and passion for missions. I used to dream of going to Africa to share the love of Christ. As our family grew, however, I began to wonder if maybe I was just supposed to be raising my children for mission trips, rather than pursuing them myself. So I passed my dream along to them. Gregg has been to Mexico. Cassie has been to Haiti, Africa, and India. Carissa and Lindsey have been to Costa Rica and Mexico. They have enjoyed their travels and have dreams of more exotic places that the Lord may lead them to.

While some of the children have traveled abroad, our family vacations and holidays have been limited to road trips. And we've had some great ones over the years. This past summer, however, we began talking about going on a family mission trip to Costa Rica. I was excited! Although we would spend time doing missions work, I was really looking forward to the beautiful condominium we were going to rent, the sunshine in the middle of winter, and the beautiful beaches to play on with the children and walk along with my husband. It was going to be the Perfect Family Holiday.

Before making our plane reservations and renting the condo, however, I discovered that my children, and the Lord, had other ideas. Rather than being excited about the beaches of Costa Rica, I discovered that the Lord had called my children's hearts to the people of New Orleans.

I do admit, though, that it probably is my fault. When we were planning our cross-country road trip for this past summer, I thought it would be nice to work in New Orleans for three days. We toured the city and were in shock at the devastation that remained a year after Katrina. We did some painting at a church. And we worked at the St. Bernard Parish distribution center. Our time there was good. We all had compassion for the people living there. We all enjoyed working at Pastor Jon's church. And, we all talked about coming back "some day." But, I didn't know that "some day" would replace the beaches of Costa Rica.

Please don't think I am complaining. I am just truly humbled that my children would ask to spend their entire two-week vacation ministering in New Orleans. We won't be walking on the beach or swimming in the surf in Costa Rica. We won't be snow skiing in Colorado or shopping in New York. We won't be enjoying a luxurious condominium.

We will be walking the streets of the city, going door-to-door, giving presents to children, praying with parents, and inviting everyone to a few events. We will be hosting a tea for ladies and The Best Party Ever (a two-day event) for children. We will be doing construction projects and working at the distribution center. We will be sharing the love of Christ with the people of New Orleans. I know that, for our family, this will be the Perfect Family Holiday.

As you begin planning your summer vacation, I encourage you to think outside the box. Rather than asking, "Where do I want to go? Where does my husband want to go? What do my kids want to do?" maybe, as a family, you should all be asking, "Where does Jesus want us to go?" When you allow Him to plan the itinerary, you can be assured that it will be the Perfect Holiday for your family.

(Note: This family just contacted me, and they have just adopted three children from Ghana, Africa, to add to their ten biological kids!

That will make seven boys and six girls in their big mission-minded family!)

Long-Term Missions

Living long term in a foreign country is much different from visiting during a short-term trip. Cultural differences, which previously were amusing and fascinating, may become extremely frustrating.

Short-term outreaches often focus on high-impact evangelism or projects that can be thrilling and encouraging. Long-term missionary work often focuses on the nitty-gritty—much needed but often not as exciting—work of discipleship training, tedious translation work, or church planting. Even the task of raising your family in another country is a time-consuming (and vitally important) ministry in itself.

As you prepare to make a move overseas, be sensitive about your standard of living. Material possessions often can be the biggest hindrance to your witness. It is easier said than done—and sometimes not feasible—but usually the best way to reach a people is to live among them with a similar, yet sanitary, standard of living.

In our travels, my husband and I have seen Western missionaries supposedly "suffering for the Lord" in conditions far beyond what they could afford back home. One time we were driving with a local pastor in a large Asian city. As we passed a neighborhood of huge, extravagant houses—each with a walled gate and several personal guards—we asked if these were homes of important government officials.

"No," he answered, "this is where most of the American missionaries live."

We were shocked; but over the years we have seen this situation repeatedly. Sometimes new missionaries may not have a choice in the matter, since many agencies and denominations have overseas housing already provided.

Fourteen Barrels and Two Large Crates

A young family went to live overseas. Their baggage did not arrive, so they had to make do with what they could find. They began developing relationships with the local people and started their missionary work.

After four months of successful ministry, their bags finally arrived. Consisting of fourteen barrels and two large crates, it was like Christmas in the summer. However, the arrival of their things brought isolation from the people they were trying to reach. Their "shipment of blessings" brought a tremendous barrier that actually hindered their work.

It's a challenge, but the fact remains: to reach a group of people effectively, a missionary must learn to live among them.

When our family travels overseas, we usually stay with nationals—eating, bathing, washing clothes, sleeping, etc., like they do. We have also stayed with many long-term missionary families that generously open their homes and their hearts to us. At times, missionary families need to facilitate large groups of foreign visitors, which usually requires more-spacious-than-normal living quarters and a higher living standard than the local people. Sometimes a missionary's home may be large, but continually shared with others. Continual hospitality is a challenge in itself.

Poverty is not a virtue, but we must be led by the Lord and by His law of love. Throughout history, the missionaries who have had the greatest impact on societies generally were those who learned to identify with the local people and not isolate themselves in a much higher social class. If God calls you and your family overseas, may He pour His blessings upon you—especially in the areas of spiritual favor and extra grace. May you and your children be blessed with God's faith, hope, and love . . . and may you fulfill all the plans He has for you.

FROM GREENLAND'S ICY MOUNTAINS

A missions hymn, by Reginald Heber (1783–1826)

From Greenland's icy mountains,
From India's coral strand;
Where Afric's sunny fountains
Roll down their golden sand:
From many an ancient river,
From many a palmy plain,
They call us to deliver
Their land from error's chain.

Shall we, whose souls are lighted
With wisdom from on high
Shall we to men benighted
The lamp of life deny?
Salvation! O Salvation!
The joyful sound proclaim,
Till earth's remotest nation
Has learned Messiah's name.

WHO WILL GO?

A missions poem, by James A. Barney

Hark! I hear a voice from o'er the waters
'Tis the cry of anguish and despair,
'Tis the cry of precious souls in darkness,
While waiting for the light of Jesus there:

Hear the idle laborers near us saying,
"Master, what wilt Thou have us to do?"
The harvest now is great!
Oh haste, my brother!
The reapers—few!

Will you go and tell them of a Savior;
Tell them how He suffered on the tree?
Will you give your very life to save them?
And tell them Jesus died to set them free?
Will you take the way, endure the suffering;
Finding in the Cross your only rest?
For suffering here with Jesus brings the glory.
His ways are best.

Who will go? Who will go?
To the ends of the earth
Hast thou a passion for the lost?
Dost thou realize what a soul is worth?
Who will go? Who will go?
Tell of Jesus' death upon the tree;
Oh, who will answer quickly,
"Here am I, Oh Lord, send me!"

We will follow, we will follow Jesus.
Willingly and gladly we'll obey.
He will never leave us nor forsake us;
He is our Friend, our Comforter and stay!
Though He lead us
O'er the briny ocean;
Though He lead us
O'er the sandy plains;
We will trust in Jesus Christ our Savior.
Oh, praise His Name!
After we've received the Spirit's fullness,

Filling all our hearts with love divine;
We're to witness to this blessed Gospel,
In every nation, country, land and clime.
When we give the Gospel as a witness
Unto every people far and near;
With lightning flash,
We'll see in clouds of glory
The King appear!

ARE YOU CALLED?

A final word, by Keith Green

It's not God's fault that the world isn't being won. It's not His will that any should perish. There's a little command in the Bible that says, "Go ye into all the world and preach the gospel to every creature."

We like to think that was for the disciples, for the missionaries, for old ladies that can't find husbands that need to bury their troubles on the mission field, or for humanitarians, for real Christians that are so spiritual they can't stay in society so they go overseas. . . . The world isn't being won because we're not doing it. It's our fault. Nowhere on earth is the gospel as plentiful as it is here in the United States. You don't need a call—you've already had one. If you stay here, you better be able to say to God, "You called me to stay home." If you don't have a definite call to stay here, you are called to go.

WHO WAS KEITH GREEN?

Keith Green was a popular Christian musician whose ministry had an impact for world missions. During his concerts, he consistently emphasized "No compromise" and "Get right with God." At the end of his life this focus went one step further to the importance of reaching the lost, especially overseas.

Only weeks before the fateful plane crash in which Keith and two of his children died, Keith and his wife, Melody, together with Loren and Darlene Cunningham of YWAM, interceded for world missions. Keith fervently cried to God for the lost and prayed that God would use him to raise up thousands of young missionaries. The words above, filled with passion and urgency, were spoken at one of his last concerts and later repeated by video at Keith Green Memorial Concerts across the United States, and multitudes responded to the call.

Today, the former property of Green's Last Days Ministries is the mission headquarters for Teen Mania Ministries, where thousands of young people from around the world are trained in missions and sent throughout the world. Keith Green's songs continue to inspire many, especially "Asleep in the Light" (based on William Booth's classic vision, "Who Cares?" about drowning lost souls).

— 👫 FROM MY CHILDREN'S PERSPECTIVE —

SHARING GOOD NEWS
By Joshua Dunagan, at age ten

I was interviewed after my first mission trip to Africa, and our local newspaper, the *Dalles Chronicle*, printed this feature article. I saw it as a chance to share the gospel at home and was excited when the editor included my comments about Jesus!

First sermon exciting for 10-year-old

■ By DAVID CLEAR
for the Chronicle

The music from the African choir and drums has scarcely died down as Joshua Dunagan steps onto a makeshift platform made of wooden planks.

Before him stretches a sea of dark-skinned faces, clad in a rainbow of colors. The people - 10,000 of them at least - wait quietly and intently. Beyond the mass of people is the desert-like prairie of northern Uganda.

Joshua, 10, is about to preach his first sermon. On a mission trip with his parents, Jon and Ann Dunagan of The Dalles, Joshua is about to experience a moment that, until now, he's only been able to dream about. He grips the microphone and lays his Bible and notebook on a small, wooden pulpit.

"I want to tell you about the most important person in the world," Joshua begins, and for the next several minutes this 10-year-old with short-cropped brown hair and a big grin tells his audience about the life of Jesus Christ and the Christian beliefs of salvation and eternity in heaven. His message is interpreted by a native Ugandan woman, and as the words are conveyed in their language, the attentive listeners break into smiles and applause.

It was a moment Joshua doesn't think he'll ever forget.

"I was excited and happy," he says, though he admits he was "a little nervous the first time. They listened so attentively, and I had all the time I wanted."

His first speech was on the life of Jesus. On another night he

spoke on the life of fiery prophet Elijah, an Old Testament figure known for performing miracles.

All his life Joshua has dreamed of going on a mission trip with his parents. As a small child he traveled with his family to several countries in Asia and Latin America, but the trip to Uganda in November of last year was his official mission trip. "It's something I've dreamed about for years," he says.

He's been influenced by his missionary parents, Jon and Ann Dunagan, founders of Harvest Ministry. Since 1987 the Dunagans have led more than 100 city-wide evangelistic crusades in remote areas overseas. The couple moved their headquarters from Bend to The Dalles last year where they're raising and homeschooling their six children. About four times a year Jon travels to Africa, India, the Philippines or some other part of the world to hold a crusade. When he can, he takes Ann and another member of the family. When they're home the family attends Covenant Christian Community Church.

For Joshua, the mission has been a long time in the making. For years he's viewed pictures and videos of his parents' mission trips, and even met guests from Africa, India and Russia that the Dunagans have hosted in their home. All of this has kindled a flame of desire in Joshua to travel to a foreign country.

When he got the OK from his father to go on the Uganda trip, Joshua immediately began preparing. He outlined several sermons and Bible lessons, or-

HERE HE IS seen in action, preaching his first sermon in the city of Koboko, Uganda.

dered his passport, and visited a doctor to get shots to protect himself from malaria, yellow fever and a host of other diseases prevalent in Uganda.

The three-week adventure began Nov. 12 at SeaTac International Airport in Seattle. The Dunagans flew to London and spent three days in Europe to adjust to the change in time zones. While there they visited popular tourist sites such as Big Ben and Buckingham Palace.

From there they then flew to the metropolitan city of Kampala, Uganda, then squeezed into a single engine Missionary Aviation Fellowship (M.A.F.) bush plane for a two-hour flight to Arua. Then came the final leg, a planned two-hour van ride to Koboko, a remote village near the border of Sudan and Congo that took four hours because of muddy roads.

For five days the Dunagans held crusade meetings in the evenings and adult and children's seminars in the mornings. While more than a thousand adults gathered to hear the morning teachings, Joshua and Ann taught Bible lessons to 300 children under a group of mango trees. Joshua schooled his Ugandan peers on the 10 Commandments and the story of Jesus.

While the work in Uganda was serious and consuming, Joshua found time for fun. He played with Uganda children, and learned the trick of putting chickens to sleep. The team also spent a day on a

wildlife safari to the Queen Elizabeth National Park. "I saw tons of animals," Joshua said, including more than 60 elephants, hundreds of hippos, an alligator, water bucks and African kobs (a type of deer). He also took a 45-minute canoe ride to Bussi Island on Lake Victoria.

But the business of meeting people's spiritual and physical needs was foremost in the mind of this delegation from The Dalles. Like Jesus, Joshua's heart swelled with compassion as he saw multitudes of needy people. Poverty is extreme in northern Uganda. Large families are crammed into 12-foot by 12-foot huts with mud floors. Disease is rampant, and scores of Sudanese refugees who have crossed the border to escape war are ravaged by years of fighting. Hundreds are blind and lame or have distortions and growths on their bodies. The children are dressed in rags.

"I've never seen so many poor and sick people," Joshua said. "Seeing people living in little huts with practically nothing made me a lot more thankful for what I have here in America."

The trip may have imprinted Joshua for life. He wants to return to Africa some day to communicate God's love to the people in any way he can. "I care about the people of the world now. They need God as much as we do I'm more willing to do whatever God wants me to do with my life."

10-YEAR-OLD Joshua Dunagan is seen at the equator in Uganda in Africa.

Conclusion

God has a destiny for your family.

He has an individual plan for each member, as well as a corporate purpose for you as a family unit. Psalm 127:4 says, "Like arrows in the hand of a warrior, so are the children of one's youth." God wants you to "aim" each of your children, and your family, toward the "bull's-eye" of His purpose. But a powerful bow must be strong and fastened tightly on two ends. As a mission-minded family, your family's "bowstring" must be aligned to biblical priorities, with two passions in balance: God has a passion for your home (including your personal relationships with Him), and God has a passion for your world.

As your family focuses on these two priorities, your home will begin to function as God intended. As a mission-minded family, you'll sense a growing, God-infused energy. You'll have worldwide purpose, and you'll have passion for the lost. Even among your children and teenagers, there will be a spiritual depth and hunger that will reach beyond the maintenance mode of cultural Christianity. You'll emphasize leadership, calling, and destiny. You'll have a prevailing attitude of self-sacrifice and a desire for total submission to God's will. And in your home (and wherever God sends you) there will be an unmistakable and contagious joy.

Psalm 112:1–2 says, "Praise the LORD! Blessed is the man who fears the LORD, who delights greatly in His commandments. His descendants will be mighty on earth; the generation of the upright will be blessed." As you follow God's mission-minded priorities, may this promise be true for you.

May you release your family to God's destiny!

Recommended Resources

Mission-Minded Prayer

- *Kids' Prayer Cards* (Caleb Project, 2006). More than just cards, this pack is a window into the lives of kids around the world! Discover what they think is fun, exciting, and cool with these twenty-five colorful cards. People Group Cards give you a look at the lives of kids in different cultures, and Activity Cards give you everything you need to paint tribal art, eat their food, and even meet and make friends with internationals in your own neighborhood. This prayer card set is built on the THUMB acrostic, and the cards are shaped like the letters: T is for Tribal, H is for Hindu, U is for Unreligious, M is for Muslim, and B is for Buddhist. Available from Caleb Resources: www.calebproject.org.

- *Operation World: 21st Century Edition*, by Patrick Johnstone and Jason Mandryk (Authentic Publishing, 2001). With over two million copies in print, this handbook for global prayer is highly recommended as a resource for mission-minded families. Packed with information about every country in the world, this book is inspiring fuel for prayer.

- *Window on the World*, by Daphne Spraggett and Jill Johnstone (Lion Hudson, Ltd., 2002 by Authentic Publishing). This children's accompaniment to *Operation World* is an outstanding tool for parents and teachers and my number one recommendation for your family. Filled with stunning full-color glossy photographs, this A-to-Z guide to one hundred countries and people groups will provide an exciting learning experience and tool for prayer.

- *Personal Prayer Diary and Daily Planner* (YWAM Publishing, 2005). Every year YWAM produces a new daily planner, which includes illustrations of unreached people, highlights for prayer, maps, monthly calendars, and Scriptures. This is an excellent organizational tool for older children, teens, and adults.

- *Walking with God: The Young Person's Prayer Diary*, by Michelle Drake (YWAM Publishing, 2005). This energetic diary will encourage your child to establish the mission-minded discipline of daily prayer. With cartoon illustrations, practical Bible-reading charts, world maps, prayer teaching highlights, and plenty of encouraging spaces for a young person to write, this tool is child friendly and highly recommended.

- *From Akebu to Zapotec*, by June Hathersmith and Alice Roder (Wycliffe Bible Translators, 2002). This second alphabet book introduces children to twenty-six of the world's Bible-less people groups. Today most of the twenty-six people groups from Wycliffe's first alphabet book, *From Arapesh to Zuni*, published in 1986, have some part of the Bible in their language—demonstrating that prayer is powerful!

- *God's Got Stuff to Do! And He Wants Your Help* (Caleb Project, 2003). This thirteen-week curriculum was created to expose kids to what can be done to help share Jesus with the nations. It includes a teacher's resource kit and a student booklet (a journal-style Bible study that leads kids to discover opportunities to go, send others, pray, give, welcome internationals in this country, and connect with others for service). Also available are *Kids Around the World* curriculum sets and the *THUMB Teacher's Resource Kit*. Available from Caleb Resources: www.calebproject.org.

- World Prayer Team, current information for international prayer: www.worldprayerteam.org

- Dare to Be a Daniel (D2BD): www.daretobeadaniel.com

- The Voice of the Martyrs: www.persecution.com

International Ministry and Ideas

- Mission-Minded International Decorations:

  Oriental Trading Company: www.orientaltrading.com

- Mission-Minded Music:

  Wee Sing Around the World (especially the song "Hello to All the Children of the World"), by Pamela Conn Beall and Susan Hagen Nipp (Price Stern Sloan, 2006)

  "Heart to Change the World" (*Kids' Praise! 6*): www.psalty.com

- Mission-Minded Drama Ministry:

  "Asleep in the Light," by Keith Green: www.lastdaysministries.org

  "The Champion," by Carman: www.carman.org

- Puppet Ministry:

  Puppet Productions (Puppetry-training DVDs, recommended songs "Laughing Song" and "Let's Go to the Church," and Spanish puppet skits): www.puppetproductions.com

- International Information:

  Country profiles and world maps: National Geographic: www.nationalgeographic.com

  Geography and history: Geography Matters: www.geomatters.com

  International embassies: www.embassy.org

  International time zones: www.timeanddate.com/worldclock

  The World Factbook: www.cia.gov/cia/publications/factbook

Mission-Minded Evangelism Tools

- *Good News Comic Book*, an excellent children's evangelism tract: www.ccci.org/good-news

- *Steps to Peace with God* (small tract), by Billy Graham Evangelistic Association (1998): www.billygraham.org/Grason.asp

- The *EvangeCube*: big cubes, small cubes, training tools and DVD, and outstanding gospel tracts in many languages. One of the most powerful evangelism tools available: www.evangecube.org

- *The Four Spiritual Laws*, by Bill Bright (Campus Crusade for Christ). Available online in almost every language. An excellent resource for international one-to-one witnessing: www.4laws.com/laws/languages.html

- The *JESUS* film, the powerful film of Jesus based on the Gospel of Luke. Over six billion exposures globally and available in nearly a thousand languages: www.jesusfilm.org

- Wycliffe Bible Translators; this premier Bible translation ministry also has many outstanding mission training books and tools for children: www.wycliffe.org

- *Planet Word Bible* (Thomas Nelson, 2005). This is my all-time favorite mission-minded Bible! It's for kids and families that want to put their faith into action. Using the NKJV translation, this Bible is filled with energetic encouragement for reaching the world. The theme is based on the GPS (Global Positioning System) of pinpointing any location in the world using four coordinates. *Planet Word* highlights four "P" Coordinates: Purpose, Power, People, and Partnership. It features 140 "Planet Messengers" (from the Bible and history), 50 "Planet Impacts" (short first-person stories of real mission-minded kids), 50 "Planet Verses" (which show Mark 1:1–4 in different languages), plus "God's Plan" introductions to every book, colorful world maps, and much more. I give this outstanding tool my highest recommendation!

- Family mission opportunities:

Adventures In Missions: www.adventures.org

Global Expeditions: www.globalexpeditions.com

Operation Christmas Child: www.samaritanspurse.org

Teen Mania: www.teenmania.com

Teen Missions: www.teenmissions.org

YWAM (Youth With A Mission): www.ywam.org and

YWAM King's Kids International: www.kkint.net

ShortTermMissions.com: www.shorttermmissions.com

(Note: These are just a sampling of the many mission opportunities available. Look on the Internet for more possibilities, and talk with your pastor or church organization for specific short- or long-term mission outreaches that could be of specific interest to your family.)

Notes

Chapter 1

Calcutta, India, analogy: special thanks to a favorite Bible teacher and friend, Bo Stern, who allowed me to adapt her analogy.

"Pursuing God's Purposes": excerpted (with minor variations) from *The Missions Addiction: Capturing God's Passion for the World*, by David Shibley (Lake Mary, FL: Charisma House, 2001), 29–30. Used with permission.

"We've a Story to Tell to the Nations": H. Ernest Nichol, 1862–1928. Words of this hymn are in public domain.

Chapter 2

Funeral example: from *The Seven Habits of Highly Effective People: Restoring the Character Ethic*, by Stephen R. Covey (New York: Simon and Schuster, 1989), 96–97.

Recommended Resource: *God's Smuggler—35th Anniversary Edition*, by Brother Andrew, John Sherrill, and Elizabeth Sherrill (Grand Rapids: Baker, 1991).

"The Call for Reapers": John O. Thompson, 1782–1818. Words of this hymn are in public domain.

Chapter 3

"The Difficult Dilemma of Jonathan Goforth": from *Goforth of China*, by Rosalind Goforth (Grand Rapids: Zondervan, 1937), 189.

"Divine Order for Each Day": from *Extravagant Worship*, by Darlene Zschech (Grand Rapids: Baker, 2004). Used with permission.

"Farewell to the Balanced Life": from *The Missions Addiction: Capturing God's Passion for the World*, by David Shibley (Lake Mary, FL: Charisma House, 2001), 78–79. Used with permission.

Chapter 4

1. Sources for Perpetua monologue: *From Jerusalem to Irian Jaya: A*

Biographical History of Christian Missions, by Ruth A. Tucker (Grand Rapids: Zondervan, 1983), 32–34; Edith Deen, *Great Women of the Christian Faith* (New York: Harper & Row, 1959), 6; Mark Galli, *131 Christians Everyone Should Know* (Nashville: B & H Publishing Group, 2000), available at http://www.christianitytoday.com/history/special/131christians/perpetua.html; Elliott Wright, *Holy Company: Christian Heroes and Heroines* (New York: Macmillan, 1980), 236.

2. Sources for John Eliot monologue: Tucker, *From Jerusalem to Irian Jaya*, 74–79; Galli, *131 Christians Everyone Should Know*, available at http://www.christianitytoday.com/history/special/131christians/johneliot.html.

3. John R. Weinlick, *Count Zinzendorf* (Nashville: Abingdon, 1956), 225.

4. Tucker, *From Jerusalem to Irian Jaya*, 116.

5. Quoted in Tucker, *From Jerusalem to Irian Jaya*, 119.

6. Tucker, *From Jerusalem to Irian Jaya*, 119.

7. Quoted in Tucker, *From Jerusalem to Irian Jaya*, 119.

8. Quoted in Deen, *Great Women of the Christian Faith*, 193–94.

9. Cecil Northcott, *Robert Moffat: Pioneer in Africa, 1817–1870* (London: Lutterworth, 1961), 189.

10. Quoted in Deen, *Great Women of the Christian Faith*, 187.

11. Tucker, *From Jerusalem to Irian Jaya*, 150.

12. Tucker, *From Jerusalem to Irian Jaya*, 153.

13. Deen, *Great Women of the Christian Faith*, 193–94; Oliver Ransford, *David Livingstone: The Dark Interior* (New York: St. Martin's, 1978), 118.

14. The story about God's provision of food for breakfast is in George Müller's own words; from *The Life and Ministry of George Müller*, a booklet by Ed Reese (Christian Hall of Fame Series, Reese Publications, Lansing, IL), available at http://www.uvm.edu/~sbross/biography/muller.txt.

15. George Müller, *A Narrative of Some of the Lord's Dealing with George Müller, Written by Himself,* 2 vols. (Muskegon, MI: Dust and Ashes, 2003), 2:392–93.

16. Denny Kenaston, "William and Catherine Booth's Home Life," an article published in *The Heartbeat of the Remnant* magazine; available online at http://libertytothecaptives.net/booth_home_life.html.

17. "Rescue the Perishing": Fanny Crosby, 1820–1915. Words of this hymn are in public domain.

18. "God's Hidden Inheritance": from *Frontier Evangelism*, by T. L. Osborn (Tulsa: Osborn Foundation, 1964). Used with permission.

Current missionary biographies were checked with each minister's official ministry website, updated 2006–2007.

Chapter 5

Holiday celebrations, music, and international ideas compiled and adapted from various sources, including the following:

Bev Gunderson, *Window to India, Window to Japan,* and *Window to Mexico* (Milaca, MN: Monarch Publishing, 1988).

Mary Branson, *Fun Around the World* (Birmingham: New Hope, 1992).

Phyllis Vos Wezeman and Jude Dennis Fournier, *Joy to the World* (Notre Dame, IN: Ave Maria Press, 1992).

Ruth Finley, *The Secret Search* (Mt. Hermon, CA: Crossroads Communications, 1990).

"I Gave Myself": Author unknown. Story excerpted from *The Harvest Call,* by T. L. Osborn (Tulsa: The Voice of Faith, Inc., 1953), 61. Used with permission of Osborn International.

Quote by Bernie May excerpted from the second edition of *From Jerusalem to Irian Jaya,* by Ruth A. Tucker (Grand Rapids: Zondervan, 2004), 391.

Chapter 6

Sources and ideas for this chapter from the author's personal experience in prayer, along with the following sources:

Danny Lehman, *Before You Hit the Wall* (Seattle: YWAM Publishing, 1991).

James P. Shaw, senior editor, *Personal Prayer Diary and Daily Planner* (Seattle: YWAM Publishing, 1995), 12–15, 192.

Chapter 7

Special acknowledgment goes to Betty Barnett and the excellent information presented in her book, *Friend Raising: Building a Missionary Support Team That Lasts* (Seattle: YWAM Publishing, revised edition, 2002).

"Daring to Live on the Edge": from *Daring to Live on the Edge: The Adventure of Faith and Finances,* by Loren Cunningham (Seattle: YWAM Publishing, 1991), excerpted from Chapter 8, "Missions Support the Jesus Way," 87–100. Used with permission of YWAM Publishing and Loren Cunningham.

Biblical examples of giving the "firstfruits" and "tithing in advance": Exodus 34:26; Leviticus 23:9–14; Deuteronomy 26:1–15; Proverbs 3:9; Ezekiel 44:30.

"A Few Startling Financial Facts" and quote about the *Queen Mary*: from *Serving as Senders: How to Care for Your Missionaries While They Are Preparing to Go, While They Are on the Field, When They Return Home*, by Neal Pirolo (San Diego: Emmaus Road International, 1991), 77, 78, 80.

In this area of missions and family finances, I highly recommend *Money, Possessions, and Eternity*, by Randy Alcorn (Tyndale, 2003).

Chapter 8

Special thanks to my precious prayer partner, Nanci Miller, for sharing her "Four Rules of Ministry" for children and for inspiring my children to be mighty lions for God, not only in ministry but also in their personal relationship with Him.

Chapter 9

"Go Ye into All the World": James McGranahan, 1840–1907. Words of this hymn are in public domain.

"From Greenland's Icy Mountains": Reginald Heber, 1783–1826. Words of this hymn are in public domain.

"Who Will Go?": James A. Barney. Original source unknown. Poem found in *The Harvest Call*, by T. L. Osborn (Tulsa: The Voice of Faith, Inc., 1953), 6. Used with permission of Osborn International.

"Are You Called?": excerpted from *Winning God's Way*, by Loren Cunningham (Seattle: YWAM Publishing, 1988), 52–53. I also recommend reading *Why You Should Go to the Mission Field*, a tract Keith Green wrote shortly before his death; available online at http://www.lastdaysministries.org/nations/whyyoushouldgo.html. For a tract catalog or to order this article in tract form, contact Last Days Ministries at 825 College Blvd. Suite 102 #333, Oceanside, CA 92057-6258 (toll-free fax 1-877-228-9536) (Ref. #043).

Illustration
Credits

Brother Andrew	Open Doors with Brother Andrew. Used with permission. All rights reserved.
Bonnke	Christ for All Nations. Used with permission. All rights reserved.
Catherine Booth	The Salvation Army International Heritage Centre. Used with permission. All rights reserved.
William Booth	The Salvation Army International Heritage Centre. Used with permission. All rights reserved.
Carey	The Christian Hall of Fame. Canton Baptist Temple, Canton, OH. Used with permission. All rights reserved (nontransferable).
Fanny Crosby	Public domain
Eliot	Public domain
Goforth	Public domain
Good News	From *The Dalles Chronicle*. Article by David Clear.
Judsons	The Christian Hall of Fame. Canton Baptist Temple, Canton, OH. Used with permission. All rights reserved (nontransferable).
Livingstone	Public domain
Moffat	Public domain
Müller	Public domain
Osborns	Osborn International. Used with permission. All rights reserved.
Patrick	The Christian Hall of Fame. Canton Baptist Temple, Canton, OH. Used with permission. All rights reserved (nontransferable).

Richardson	Don Richardson. Used with permission. All rights reserved.
Studds	Public domain
Whitmans	Adaptation of two public domain images
Zinzendorf	Public domain
Darlene Zschech	Hillsong Church. Used with permission. All rights reserved.

For more information about the author (and more mission-minded ideas for your family, including free online mission resources), please visit Harvest Ministry at www.harvestministry.org and Daring Daughters at daringdaughters.org. Founded by Jon and Ann Dunagan in 1987, Harvest Ministry focuses on winning souls, loving orphans, equipping nationals, serving churches, and motivating mission-minded families.

Special thanks to my wonderful husband, Jon, and to our children: Patrick, Joshua, Christi, Daniel, Mark, Caela, and Philip. I love you all!

World Maps

Special thanks to Josh and Cindy Wiggers of Geography Matters (www.geomatters.com) for designing the following world maps.

AFRICA

©2009 Geography Matters   www.geomatters.com

ICELAND

Norwegian Sea

SWEDEN

NORWAY

FINLAND

Gulf of Bothnia

North
Atlantic
Ocean

ESTONIA

Baltic Sea

RUSSIA

LATVIA

North Sea

DENMARK

LITHUANIA

IRELAND

RUSSIA

NETHERLANDS

U.K.

BELARUS

POLAND

GERMANY

English Channel

BELGIUM

UKRAINE

LUX.

CZECH
REP.

Caspian
Sea

FRANCE

SLOVAKIA

AUSTRIA

MOLDOVA

SWITZERLAND

HUNGARY

Bay of Biscay

ROMANIA

SLOVENIA

CROATIA

Black Sea

BOSNIA

PORTUGAL

ANDORRA

SERBIA

ITALY

CORSICA

Adriatic

BULGARIA

MONTENEGRO

SPAIN

MACEDONIA

SARDINIA

BALEARIC
ISLANDS

Tyrrhenian Sea

ALBANIA

GREECE

TURKEY

Aegean

SICILY

Ionian Sea

MALTA

Mediterranean Sea

all rights reserved

EUROPE

©2005 Geography Matters www.geomatters.com

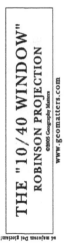

THE "10/40 WINDOW"
ROBINSON PROJECTION
©2005 Geography Matters
www.gcomatters.com

¡al mejoran Del gloriam!

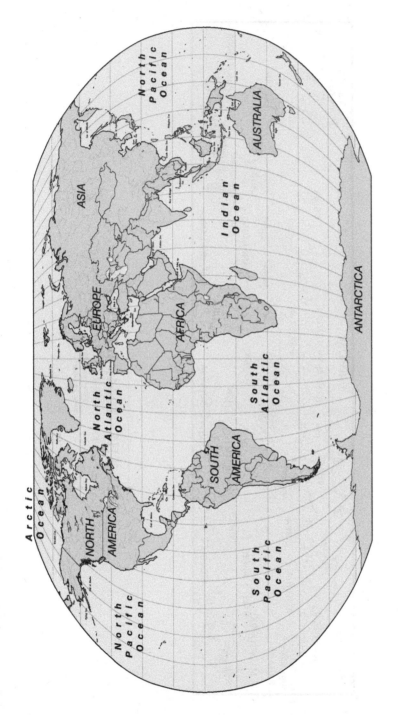

THE WORLD
ROBINSON PROJECTION
©2005 Geography Matters